Inch by Inch

Finding a Home within My Skin

Monique Lisbon

Includes full album of MP3
song downloads by the author

Published in 2020 by Living Hope Resources
PO Box 324 Ashburton Victoria 3147 Australia
www.livinghoperesources.com.au
www.inchbyinch.net.au

Book © Monique Lisbon 2020
Album © Monique Lisbon and Adrian Hannan 2020

The right of Monique Lisbon to be identified as the author of this book has been asserted in accordance with the Copyright Act 1968 (Australia). No part of this publication may be reproduced, stored in a retrieval system, or transmitted, in any form or by any means, electronic, mechanic, photocopying, recording or otherwise, without the prior written permission of the publisher.

Editor: Trudy Skilbeck

Book and cover design: Monique Lisbon, Mono Unlimited

National Library of Australia Cataloguing-in-Publication entry:

ISBN: 978-0-6481250-3-7 (paperback + downloadable MP3s)

A catalogue record for this book is available from the National Library of Australia

*For 'Bethany' –
the compassionate holder of my scales*

*And for all those who have held my heart
as you have held the hope
for a better future for me*

Contents

Foreword by Dr Diana Kelly-Byrne vi

Introduction 1

1   His Property 3

2   A Practised Blind Eye 13

3   Etched in My Skin 27

4   Escaping My Skin 37

5   Stuck 47

6   In My Shoes 57

7   Skin on Skin 67

8   The Turning Point 83

9   Finding My Feet 93

10   Learning to Fly 105

11   A Tender Dance 115

Song Download Details & Credits 127

- Foreword -

The traumatic effects of childhood abuse are overwhelming. They can imprison the victim for years in cycles of depression, anxiety, dissociation, somatisation, self-injury, suicidal attempts, insomnia, hypervigilance, risky behaviour, body dysmorphia and other life-denying, self-loathing behaviours.

Healing occurs in stages. Recovery is hard-won and takes courage. The links between morbid obesity and child abuse are well documented.[1]

Inch by Inch can proudly take its place among reports of women victims of childhood sexual abuse and their individual journeys toward healing. It is the third account by the writer to chronicle the stages of her healing.

Sexual abuse is never just something that happened in the past. It seeps into the body, mind and soul of the victim and is forever part of their life. This text focusses on the victim's experience of how, in various manifestations, we are our bodies. As a leading trauma expert reminds us, 'the body keeps the score'.[2]

Monique's fear, confusion and overwhelming need for protection from unspeakable assaults on her little body was not

---

[1] Vincent Fellitti, 'Adverse Childhood Experiences Study', quoted in Olga Khazan, 'The Second Assault', 15 December 2015, www.theatlantic.com/health/archive/2015/12/sexual-abuse-victims-obesity/420186/, accessed 18 August 2020.

[2] Bessel van der Kolk, *The Body Keeps the Score: Mind, Brain and Body in the Transformation of Trauma* (Penguin Books: 2015).

met with the comfort of safe motherly arms. Instead, her terror was assuaged by rewards of strawberry tarts from her abusive father. She discovered that her deep hunger for love was quelled by the comfort of chocolate, devoured in secret. The sensory pleasure of food soothed her anxiety. It became a guilty solace.

Neuroimaging of the brain reveals how our fundamental needs for love, connection, safety and nurture become mired in confused and distorted images and behaviours, when those whom we are programmed to love, hurt us. It can also be the case that the abused victim's relationship to food becomes disordered.

Monique illustrates how her struggle with weight and eventual morbid obesity played out in her life and relationships from childhood to the present. Of note is the course of her struggle to wrest her body back from her mother. Monique was given the message that her mother wanted her to literally disappear. She thoughtfully reflects that her obesity was a silent challenge to her mother, saying, in effect, 'I'm not going anywhere.'

Her prior book, *Keeping Mum*[3], was not only about the ways her father's coercive threats, and her mother's denial, kept her 'mum'. The figure of speech also speaks to Monique's yearning for her mother's love and approval. Unfortunately it kept her stuck in an erratic dance with her weight. This would continue as long as she sought to keep [her] mum.

Reaching the hard-won decision to walk out of these imprisoning relationships with her family, one at a time, over a fifteen-year period, was crucial to her liberation. Then, as with many who walk free from imprisonment, there is much work to be done on the other side. Learning to be free is no mean feat.

Attempts to engage with the pain and shame lodged deep within layers of fat and to risk trusting one's body as a place of safety and even desire, were fundamental precedents to Monique embarking on the road of re-claiming and re-imagining her body for herself. It is a tale of homecoming, of embracing all of her shattered self and

---

3   Monique Lisbon, *Keeping Mum: The Silent Cost of Surviving Childhood Sexual Abuse* (Living Hope Resources: Ashburton, Victoria, 2017).

the challenge of feeling safe in her body.

This is an intelligently written and careful account. It is raw, honest and pulls no punches. As a reader, it invites you in quickly and smacks you into the heart of the victim's experience as she moves from childhood, through latency, adolescence, young adulthood and through to middle age. As if in a movie, the camera moves from the plight of a small helpless child, shocked into speechless terror to a woman who carried her pain and protest in massive mounds of flesh that threatened to seriously disable her; a living reminder of the cruel damaging of her tender life and spirit, so ruthlessly robbed from her.

Monique's abuse and stress reactions, if triggered, will always tug at her. Nevertheless, today their power is diminished, particularly as now she is held in her own deep embrace.

This chronicle exemplifies the ways in which Monique authored and became the arbiter of her own recovery, with her characteristic grit and determination, as she walked, step-by-step, to come home to herself; a quest full of grace and truth.

– Dr Diana Kelly-Byrne PhD
Psychologist (Melbourne, Australia)

- Introduction -

I lived for decades in a land shaped by humiliation, shame, disgust, alienation, immobility, hatred, judgment and powerlessness. Initially this terrain was invisible – it was shaped in my mind and psyche, the primary loci of damage from abuse.

Yet abuse is not merely conceptual or abstract. It is concrete. It occurs within the landscape of a human body.

Over time, my body grew as the nexus of the long-term damage I experienced throughout my childhood. It grew both in its power to limit and constrain me, and it grew in physical size. By the time I reached adulthood, I was well on my way to feeling powerless to ever escape the prison I carried everywhere. I had temporary jailbreaks – finding ways to flee from my body through self-denial, dissociation, fads, and intensive and unsustainable changes in lifestyle.

But one can never truly escape oneself. And it is counterproductive to try.

I have now lost nearly two-thirds of my body weight. When I look at 'before' photos, it is hard to recognise myself physically. What I do recognise is the life, determination and tenacity displayed in the eyes and smiles in those photos. Yes, the smile was genuine. There is no way I could ever have moved to this new land – one of freedom, self-respect, mobility, health, a lightness of being, even joy – without a fundamental belief in my own sense of agency and power to change.

I never want to reject the 'old' me as a source of disdain and shame – that would defeat the purpose of the transformation I have experienced. There is no 'old' and 'new' me. My body, mind

Inch by Inch

and psyche are central to who I am. They have been with me since I was born and, even as they undergo constant change, they will stay with me until I die. I look on my 'before' photos with compassion and admiration of my spirit.

My journey from morbid obesity to living health has also been a trek from self-hatred and shame, towards self-respect and freedom.

– Monique Lisbon,
August 2020

- One -

His Property

Frozen body
Waiting for your move

Frozen

Frozen body
Waiting for your move
Casting darkness
Which play will you choose?

Eyes wide open
Closing off my mind
Trusting danger
Dying to survive

Words and Music © Monique Lisbon 2008

It is late and dark when I wake up, but I can still see around my bedroom because my pink nightlight is on. Loud noises from the lounge room have woken me up. Did Mummy and Daddy leave the television on when they went to bed?

I am five years old.

I listen hard. I can hear people talking loudly. Daddy laughs and says, 'Hang on, it's my turn! And I'm going to win this round!'

They must be playing games! I know that my brother Grant is two and a half years older than me, but isn't it past his bedtime too? So why does he get to stay up and play games with Mum and Dad while I have to stay in bed and sleep? That's not fair!

I jump out of bed and put on my soft pink slippers. I want to play too! I run to the lounge room, open the two big doors, step inside and shut the doors forcefully behind me.

Then I turn to face my family.

My family is not there. I can see Daddy – but there's no sign of Mummy or Grant. Instead, there's a group of about eight men sitting around our dining table, playing cards. There's lots of cakes heaped up in the middle of the big table – creamy flaky ones, curly ones with coloured icing, thick chocolate slabs, and, my favourite, strawberry tarts.

It's really stinky in the room. All the men are smoking – not thin cigarettes like Mummy's, but big fat sticks with lots of black smoke coming out of them. Cigars.

If Daddy notices me, I'll be in trouble for getting out of bed! So I try to sneak back to the doors and open them quietly, without being seen.

Too late for that.

'Well, what do we have here? Is this part of the entertainment?' one of the men barks.

I am scared. This man is big and ugly, and he has a dark bushy beard. He stinks of smoke.

All the other men laugh and Daddy comes over to me and scoops me up in his arms. He is not angry at me like I thought he would be. He just laughs as he looks down at my face. Daddy's breath smells too – not of smoke, but with the same sort of smell he has when he and Mummy go out dancing. When they get home, Mummy says they've had a 'glass or two of red'. I don't know what that means, but I sure know what it smells like.

'Yes, we do aim to please!' Daddy says to the ugly man, and carries me over to the dining table. Then he plonks me down on the half-empty platter in the middle of the table, laughing loudly. My bottom lands in a mound of cream in the middle of the large plate and the cream gets all over my pyjamas.

Daddy pulls my pyjamas off me. Now I'm sitting there on the plate, naked; just like a big pink cake.

One of the men says, 'It was clearly worth sticking around for dessert! How much will this treat cost us?' and the others all burst out laughing.

'Well, that all depends on how much of it you devour!' says Daddy.

The men start to grab at me, poking their fingers on my chest and tummy, then inside my bottom, at the front and at the back.

Daddy watches them all playing with me, a big smile on his face. 'That's an ace in the hole!' he says.

One man picks up his cigar from the ashtray and sucks on it deeply in his mouth. Then he flicks some of the black ash onto my bare leg. It hurts and I start to cry.

'OK, I'll call you all! Time to pay up!' says Daddy. The men all flick plastic chips from the colourful piles sitting next to each of them, towards Daddy. He gathers all the chips into one huge pile and pulls them towards his edge of the table with both arms.

'Looks like I'm the winner tonight!' he brags.

I close my eyes and try to imagine being tucked safely back in bed, burying myself under the blankets in my mind.

The men's laughter starts to sound like it's a long, long way away, to the point where I can't hear anything at all.

And eventually, everything goes dark and disappears.

The next time I wake up, it is morning and I am in my bed. My pink nightlight is still on. I can hear a lawnmower purring in the neighbour's backyard.

Daddy walks into my room and says, 'Good morning! Get up and dressed. You're getting a special treat today!'

He drives me to the French cake shop. When we walk in the door, the smell is very yummy – all warm and sugary. All the same cakes are there, just like last night's party – the creamy flaky ones, the curly ones with coloured icing, the thick chocolate slabs … and, of course, the strawberry tarts.

'You deserve a special reward. You can choose whatever you want. What would you like?' Daddy asks.

I choose a strawberry tart. When Daddy pulls out his wallet to pay the man behind the counter, he gives him a five dollar bill, not one of the coloured plastic chips that he collected last night from his friends.

Somehow, without words, I know exactly what I'm being rewarded for … and exactly how it's being paid for.

And I devour my strawberry tart as though my life depended on it.

I am twelve years old.

Now that I've finished primary school, I'm very fortunate to be going to a private girls' school – that's what Sue Ellen's mother said at her birthday party at the end of last year. I wish I was going to the local high school with Sue Ellen though. She's really been my one and only friend at the end of primary school, and I'm scared that I won't be able to make friends when I get to the new school.

At my fancy private school, we have to wear our blazers over our uniforms whenever we're out in public. If we get spotted without our blazers on, we can get in trouble because the headmistress says it reflects badly on the school.

My family moved house at the end of last year, and our new home is really nice, but it just doesn't compare with the houses some of the other girls live in. Rosalie Braidwood's father is a barrister and her family lives in a mansion! It's so big that I actually get lost whenever I go there, even just trying to find my way from her bedroom with its private ensuite bathroom, past the dining room, family room, study, den, office, sewing room, exercise room, playroom, and guest room, through to the backyard!

Rosalie's family also has a holiday house on the coast, and she even has her own horse that gets looked after at a pony club!

I really like Rosalie, but I don't know why she would like me. I don't have nearly as many nice things as she does, and I can't give her the kinds of presents that she must be used to getting.

The top drawer inside Dad's wardrobe is filled with loose coins. I guess it's kind of like a grown-up money-box. Whenever Dad gets change from shopping, he throws the coins in there. I wonder how much money there would be if you ever took it all out and counted it – probably thousands of dollars! In any case, there's enough coins there that he'd never notice if I took some.

I've come up with a plan to make sure that Rosalie keeps wanting to spend time with me … and the other rich kids too.

Dad might just help me make good friends and keep them on my side.

When I walk to the tram-stop to go to school each day, I pass a milkbar. Today, I fetch a couple of coins from my father's wardrobe before I leave. Then I stop at the milkbar and buy twenty choc-buds for 2 cents each, 40 cents in total. The man at the counter of the milkbar laughs and says, 'Twenty choc-buds! That'll stop you getting hungry!'

'They're for my classmates!' I protest.

I carry the choc-buds to school with me and, at recess, I give one to each kid in my class. It's a hit!

After a couple of days of doing this, I realise that I really need to increase my gifts if they're going to keep having an effect. And even though I'm buying lots of choc-buds every day, I'm not getting to enjoy them myself.

So I start buying more choc-buds – forty each day for 80 cents, then fifty for $1.00.

On Day Five, the milkbar owner laughs out loud when I ask for sixty choc-buds. 'My goodness, your class has really grown in size in just one week, hasn't it?' he says.

I feel embarrassed and ashamed. I know I need to stop increasing the quantity I buy. So I decide to set my daily limit at sixty choc-buds.

And I also decide to stop giving them to my classmates. Instead, I make sure that I've eaten them all, well and truly, before I even get to school, and before anyone can see.

My class doesn't grow in size, but I do.

And every day, without him even knowing it, Dad is supporting my hidden, guilty, sweet secret.

I am fifteen years old.

Down the end of the street and around the corner from my house, there's a nature reserve where lots of my neighbours go walking. Unlike my mother, Dad really hates nature – he's always worried about getting dirt on his hands and clothes. Dad's kind of holiday would never involve camping – more like five-star hotels.

So when Dad says that we're going to start walking together as a family in the evenings, I know he doesn't mean walking in the reserve.

Instead, we start trekking around the streets – Mum, Dad and I. Sometimes my brother Grant also comes. I don't really like nature much, either. So it suits me that we're staying away from the reserve.

One evening, my mother starts chanting a cute little ditty on our walk.

'*Left* ... right ... *left*, right, *left*. I *left* my wife in New Orleans, with twenty-five kids and a can of beans, 'cause I thought it was *right* ... *right* ... *right* for my country ... woop-ti-do!'

As Mum says the word, 'woop-ti-do', she shuffles her feet quickly like she's dancing on the spot, so that she ends up landing on the opposite foot.

We all laugh.

'I want to give it a go!' I say, and off I trot down the street, chanting and laughing, 'I left my wife in New Orleans, with twenty-five kids and a can of beans …'

I feel a crazy kind of freedom.

Then Dad gets in on the act.

'Left … right … left … right … left … right … left … right …' he says. But he doesn't chant the rest of the ditty. Instead he just orders us to march in time to his dictation, on and on, for a very long time.

Very quickly, it stops being fun.

The next evening, when I set off on a walk alone with Dad, rather than him chanting, 'left … right … left … right …' he decides to count my steps instead.

It's impossible to think, talk, or enjoy what's around, when every step of my trip is being measured and counted out loud. I certainly can't even say anything while he's loudly chanting, 'One hundred and seventy-two … one hundred and seventy-three … one hundred and seventy-four …'

Before I know it, these daily walks become just another way in which my every move is measured, counted, judged and dictated by my father.

I am sixteen years old.

Martin is my first real boyfriend, and I've been really excited to have him in my life.

The downside is that Dad has decided that Martin is part of a cult, and that I need to be protected from him and the other friends I've made through my church youth group and a Christian horse-riding camp. So I'm forbidden from contacting them. Dad has rung some of them up, to tell them in no uncertain terms not to contact me either. He also made me break up with Martin by letter.

Dad says he knows what's best for me, and that he's going to 'deprogram' me from the ways I've been brainwashed by these dangerous religious people.

At night-time, when I'm sure Dad is asleep, I pull out my Bible from its hiding place inside my underwear drawer, and read it under the bed-covers with a torch, for comfort.

But at some point during the night, I fall asleep with my Bible open inside my bed and my torch still on. When I wake up the next morning, I realise Dad has come into my room in the middle of the night, found the Bible and taken it away.

So that source of comfort has gone now too, along with all the other things he's already taken away – my journal, letters from friends, cards from Martin, pages and pages of personal writing, all my Christian books, and my address book with all my friends' contact details.

I find something else to comfort me under the covers at night, when I'm alone.

As long as I make sure it's gone by the time I fall asleep, I won't wake up and find he's found and confiscated my source of comfort the next morning.

And it's much easier to get rid of empty tubes of sweetened condensed milk without Dad noticing, than a heavy Bible.

- Two -

A Practised Blind Eye

Your terror at facing your guilt
Your complicity, your neglect
Renders me utterly invisible

Wasting Away

Your first pay-off was to a middle-aged woman
Who nagged unhappy strangers
About resisting temptation
I learned about the boundary that must never be crossed
Mars Bars were judged 'illegal'
And the fine for my crime
Was 13 pounds withdrawn from the folds of my flesh
Still your husband kept feasting on my pre-pubescent pulp
But you were happy, and that was all that mattered
Yeah, 'cos there were 13 pounds less of me for you to see

And I was wasting away …

The cost of your next intervention
Was covered by your library membership
An encyclopaedic catalogue of diseases
Penned in your neat and concerned hand
Begging me to reverse my predicament
Only you could see the 'big fat lady' in front of you
My mid-size clothes must have tricked the world from seeing
So I set about to shed my shame
Determined I would lose so much of me
That you'd no longer recognise me

I was wasting away … wasting away …
See me wasting away … wasting away …

Four years, many diets and two suicide attempts later
What was left of me to recognise?
I thought I'd found a way to gain your approval
Weekly outings in your car
From my psychiatric bed to Jenny Craig™

I reached your goal
Eradicated half of my body
Then you said
'You put that weight back on …
And I'll shoot myself.'
I did. But you didn't

I was wasting away … wasting away …
See me wasting away … wasting away …

Two decades later I still see the disgust
As you turn a practised blind eye to this big, fat lady
Where did I come from?
From the one who chewed me up
Or the other who spat me out?
Yeah, I'm larger than life
My very body defies your demand of non-existence
Yet your terror at facing your guilt
Your complicity, your neglect
Renders me utterly invisible

Wasting away … I am wasting away … wasting away …

Words © Monique Lisbon 2014
Music © Adrian Hannan 2019

Inch by Inch

It's the second-last day of school and I have just brought home my report card. Mum and Dad are really pleased with me because I've been given straight A's for just about all of my school subjects – Maths, English, History, Geography, Art and Social Studies.

But one mark spoils the whole thing …

'How can anyone even *get* an "E" for Sport?!' Mum laughs.

I am eleven years old.

I know exactly how someone can get an 'E' for Sport. When it comes to being chosen for sports teams, I'm *always* picked last. It's like the other kids forget I'm even there when they're picking their team-mates one by one. When it's my turn, the kids on my team actually groan when my name is finally called. And the other team cheers because they're better off without me on their side.

So by the time we start playing, I already feel hopeless and ashamed. I know that it's me who makes our team lose the games and come last in the relay races. I'm so uncoordinated that I just can't catch the ball, even though I try really hard. And no matter how fast I try to run, I always end up crossing the line long after everyone else has finished.

When the teacher is not listening, the other kids laugh at me and call me 'Hippopotamus' and 'Elephant'. It really hurts because I am trying so hard to not stand out, to just be normal like everyone else.

I tell Mum about what the other kids say, and how hurt I feel by the names they call me.

'Can't you do anything to stop them?' I beg.

But Mum just laughs. 'We all have our lot in life,' she says, 'and this is yours. Just tell them, "You're no spring chicken yourself." And just laugh it off. "Sticks and stones may break my bones, but names will never hurt me."'

I don't know what a 'spring chicken' is, but I try to do what my mother tells me. The next time the kids tease me and start chanting, 'Hippopotamus, Elephant, Hippopotamus, Elephant …', I reply, 'Well, you're no spring chicken yourself!'

I don't think they know what a 'spring chicken' is either. So my words only end up making them laugh louder, and their teasing only increases.

It really, really hurts.

But Mum seems to thinks it's not an issue, so maybe I just need to learn to live with this lot in life – the lot of living as a hippopotamus.

Where can a hippopotamus go to hide?

Too Much of Me[4]

I am thirteen years old.

Before school, I show Mum an article in *Dolly*, my favourite magazine. It's about a girl who felt bad about herself so she decided to lose weight and she ate nothing but grapefruit.

Grapefruit? Yuck!

When I get home from school, Mum says, 'I was thinking about the article you showed me this morning. You know, there are better diets for you to go on than a grapefruit diet. I rang Weight Watchers today, and they've got a meeting on tonight, so I told them I'm bringing you.'

When I showed Mum the magazine this morning, I wasn't trying to say I wanted to go on a diet … and certainly not a grapefruit one.

But Mum obviously thinks I need to lose weight, so off we go.

This is my first time at Weight Watchers. I look around the

---

4 The section 'Too Much of Me' (pp. 17-24) is taken from *Keeping Mum: The Silent Cost of Surviving Childhood Sexual Abuse* by Monique Lisbon (Living Hope Resources: Ashburton, Victoria, 2017), pp 25-31.

room – a church hall. I had no idea that churches held meetings like this. I always thought that going to church was about believing in God, not about losing weight.

I'm the only kid here. In fact, I think most of the people are over 30. There's a couple of men, but mostly the room is filled with women.

We watch as the lady in charge weighs everyone. One by one, they step up onto these big scales and she moves weights back and forth to work out whether they've been good or bad this week. One lady is very upset because she has gained two pounds.

The Weight Watchers lady says, 'Well, you'd better stay away from those illegal foods this week then, hadn't you!'

What on earth are illegal foods?

Everyone sits down in rows and listens to the woman up the front. She tells us that she used to be overweight too, but Weight Watchers changed her life, so she's dedicated herself to helping others peel off the layers of fat to find their real selves.

She says, 'Just think … you'll never eat another Mars Bar again in your life.'

I guess she knows what she's talking about. I mean, this is her job. Every Monday night she is paid to come and tell people how to lose weight.

Now I realise that Mars Bars must be illegal!

I wonder what happens when you break Weight Watchers Law?

After the meeting is over, the woman weighs me. I weigh exactly 100 pounds. She asks if I've got my period yet and I tell her I haven't. She tells Mum, 'I'm not sure if Monique really qualifies to join Weight Watchers. But we'll set her goal weight at 87 pounds and she can start tonight.' Then she starts going through the booklet to explain what the legal and illegal foods are.

She says that the main things I need to do are to be disciplined and resist temptation.

I know I'm really good at being disciplined – that bit is easy. I work hard at school and get A's for everything (except for Sport!).

When it comes to resisting temptation, I'm not really sure how I'll go.

Some mornings when I'm in the shower, Grant comes into the bathroom to clean his teeth. Before he leaves, he always throws a bucket of cold water over the edge of the shower. Whenever I try to tell Mum, she just says that Grant and I only fight to get her attention, so she's not going to reward us by intervening.

It really upsets me. I know I haven't got my period yet, so I'm not officially a 'woman', but I still feel embarrassed that Grant is allowed to come into the bathroom when I'm naked, and that Mum won't do anything to stop him dumping cold water on me.

On those mornings, I go downstairs to the toilet straight after my shower. There's a toilet right next to the bathroom upstairs, but the downstairs toilet is the only room in the house with a lock, so it's the only place I can go to cry without the chance of someone walking in on me. If Dad or Grant saw me crying, they'd just tease me – and that would make it so much worse.

The downstairs toilet is also the place where I can eat chocolate in secret. After I finish crying, I take out the chocolate that I've sneaked in with me, and let the smooth sweetness melt my pain away.

Then I wrap the chocolate wrapper inside a bunch of toilet paper and flush it all away, along with everything else.

Is that giving into temptation? … or is it only temptation if people know that I'm doing it?

The big day has come. I only need to lose another half a pound and then I will have reached my goal weight. At school, I throw out the food in my lunchbox. Yes, it's all legal food – but I want to make sure that I reach my goal tonight, so I'm sure that not eating will help.

I tell Mum that I am too nervous to eat dinner, and we leave for Weight Watchers after the rest of the family has finished eating.

When I weigh in, the lady says, 'Half a pound loss – very good.' She records the loss on my card and doesn't notice that I've reached the magic number: 87.

I have been focussing on this number for six months, knowing that when I finally reach it, I will be slim. I will be happy.

The lady in charge goes around the circle and reads out each person's results for the week – how much we've each lost or gained. She passes over me quickly, and I wonder whether to point out that I have now reached my goal weight. I wait till she announces the results for three other ladies before I put up my hand and say shyly, 'Actually I reached my goal weight tonight.'

'So you did!' she says.

I am awarded with a small pendant – a round, gold badge with 'WW' on it, and a tiny diamond. This is a sign to help me remember I have finally made it!

I feel so proud of myself. I was disciplined and I resisted temptation, and I reached the goal that had been set for me.

Maybe, now that I am an official Life Member of Weight Watchers, Mum will finally be proud of me too.

I am nineteen years old.

I'm in my second year at university, and live with three friends in a shared house.

Life is good. I love the long group conversations in the uni cafeteria, discussing the meaning of life. I am enrolled in a double-major in Philosophy. One of the biggest things I've learned so far is how easy it is for lively debate to go on for five hours, without anyone reaching conclusions about how we can prove the chairs we're sitting on even exist!

Playing around with words and ideas and concepts is great. Talking about important things – what makes us tick and why it matters – is greater still.

But best of all, I've made some really good friends – people I know I'll remain close to for the rest of my life.

It is late November and my mother flew out to Switzerland this morning to spend Christmas with her family. It's the first time she's gone overseas since I moved out of home, just over a year ago.

I check the letterbox and I'm pleased to find an envelope penned with her hand. She must have written me a farewell note, to wish me a Merry Christmas, before she flew out.

The envelope does not contain the personal Christmas letter I expect. Mum has typed two pages, then signed her name at the bottom.

It looks important, so I sit down to read it:

```
My dearest Monique,

I had a cup of coffee the other day at McDonalds.  This was
10 o'clock in the morning when I had to do a message in the city.
Next to me was a young woman with two small children, one of them
being retarded.  This woman was about 22 years of age and she
was huge in size.  She tucked into two hamburgers, one big serve
of chips and an ice cream with chocolate sauce. She then drowned
everything with a big glass of drink.

This picture made me very sad as I realised that the poor woman
must be caught up in the suburban syndrome of problems with small
children, nothing to do and bingeing to pass the time or escape
from something.  Inevitably, because of the woman's size, my
thoughts go to you, my lovable daughter and I start to worry.
You have become a big fat woman too and I just feel that you should
make an effort to change your attitude for your health's sake.
You really run the risk of sugar diabetes, varicose veins and/or
hemmorhoids (this spelling is off) all of which are NOT pleasant.

Should you ever have a family, these problems could become so
painful that nobody would wish them on anybody, let alone your
favorite daughter. My dear Monique, I think now is the time to
start thinking about your shape and health.  You are no longer a
teenager and the puppy fat stage is past.  Should you decide to do
something about this present problem and shed a considerable
amount of weight, I feel sure that you will not have a weight
problem from then on as obesity is not in our family.
```

Inch by Inch

– 2 –

You will tell me that you want to be accepted as you are. I am sure that you <u>are</u> accepted as you are. This point does not have to be proven any longer. I, for one, love you dearly and I am sure so do all your friends. I respect your wishes to be a responsible grown up person. I do not feel that I have obstructed you unduly in letting you do whatever you have been doing. You may see this differently but I feel that I have always tried to encourage you, rather than hinder you.

I am immensely proud of you - you are not a disappointment in any way to me. In my own silly way I just try to do what I feel is good for you. This has nothing to do with tying you to my apron strings. You can tell me any time to buzz off, however, a mother's feelings are just like that.

One (of many) of your strong points is your determination and grit when you make up your mind to achieve something. You gave up Diet Coke for Lent, a sacrifice to say the least. Now do something for yourself, put yourself on a diet, stick to it and fitness will become very easy once your body does not have to cope with all that excessive fat. Don't say, yes yes Mum, I can guarantee you that you will feel better half your size. This will not change your character, you still have your same acute mind, you still have all your other rights to do pretty much what you decide is your way of being a responsible human being, you will still enjoy your friends, your work, your studies, your leisure, your music, however, without your health, all the above might become very much secondary.

Will you please analyse what I am saying? bearing in mind that you are <u>not</u> a lesser person to me because of the way you have let yourself go. You are <u>not</u> a lesser person to me because of your size, you are <u>not</u> a disappointment to me and I am telling you <u>not</u> to feel guilty in any way that you do not live up to my expectations. I love you von Herzen no matter what but don't tell me that you enjoy being fat because I do not think that you are a masochist.

I have resorted to putting my thoughts on paper as this is really between you and me and the rest of our family does not have to be involved.

I look forward to seeing you when I get back from Switzerland. You are the best, I love you very much.

Mum x x x x

When my housemate Jason gets home, I show him the letter. He asks how I feel about it and what I'm going to do.

I tell him, 'I've already started – I'm now officially on a diet. Mum obviously loves me very much to have written me something like this, so I want to do what she's saying.'

Jason just shakes his head, then walks out of the room without saying anything.

I'm already thinking ahead … If I can lose 1-2 kgs a week, then I'll already be a significant way towards losing half my size by the time she gets back from overseas.

I'll work hard to do her proud! She's right – I do have determination and grit. So I'll use those positive traits, once again, to do exactly what she says – to avoid feeling guilty that I do not live up to her expectations.

Of course, I'll need to buy some new clothes after I've finished, because all my current size 12 clothes[5] will hang off me like tents.

But that's a small price to pay to avoid her disappointment in me.

I am twenty-two years old.

In the last two years, the impact of my childhood abuse has hit me like a ton of bricks. I've been on a roller coaster of depression, anxiety, tormenting memories and self-harm. I've tried to kill myself several times – it's not that I want to die, I just don't know how to keep living with all this. I feel an occasional glimmer of hope, then inevitably, I plummet back into despair. I'm on truckloads of medication, yet I still have days and weeks when I can barely function. I only get out of bed to stumble to the bathroom, or to answer the door to receive my daily fast-food deliveries – cooking is impossible in this state.

A week ago, things reached such a low point that I was once again admitted to a psychiatric ward. Until today, I haven't been allowed

---

5   Australian size 12 = US size 8.

to leave the ward on my own because they're worried I might try to kill myself. Today the doctors have given me permission to leave the hospital for a couple of hours with Mum.

We don't spend our limited time together window shopping or going for a stroll in the park. Instead, she drives me straight to Jenny Craig™. I get weighed, sit through the ten-minute pep talk and receive my food parcels for the coming week. I don't tell the weight loss consultant that I'm currently a patient in a psychiatric hospital, and that my Jenny Craig™ food is being heated up each day by the hospital kitchen staff.

This time, it takes me nearly a year to reach my goal weight. Mum and I go out to celebrate. I know I'm in her good books when she buys me a new wardrobe and we perform our semi-regular ritual of giving all my old clothes to the Op Shop, to help me resist the temptation to go backwards.

Out with the old, in with the new.

This time around, her words of approval come with a threat: 'Put that weight back on and I'll shoot myself.'

Inevitably, I do.

She doesn't.

I am thirty years old.

Over the last decade I have been admitted to psychiatric hospitals more times than I care to count; on average three or four times per year, for up to a month or more at a time.

It's been hard to maintain regular work. I am fortunate that the church where I'm employed part-time allows me time off work whenever I need to go to hospital, and they hold my job open for me after I've been discharged. Naturally, when I'm not working, I don't get paid – and this can end up being for several months of the year.

Money is pretty tight. I do receive Sickness Benefits from the government, but the rate of pay is below the poverty line, so it's often hard to make ends meet.

Thankfully Mum has been very supportive of me when I've struggled financially. One of the biggest ways she helps me is by buying my clothes. I'm too big to fit into clothes from 'normal' clothes shops, so we regularly visit the fashion stores for 'big girls'. The clothes are much more expensive in these shops, but I go home with new clothes that fit, at least for a few months.

Inevitably my body keeps growing – and the clothes don't. So I end up no longer fitting into the clothes Mum bought me only months earlier.

Finally Mum draws a line in the sand. After our third shopping trip for the year, while we're waiting at the counter for her to pay for my new size 22 clothes, she says, 'I will not buy you any clothes beyond size 22.'

I know that Mum is trying to help. But it really doesn't help. I already feel trapped and unacceptable. I can't afford to buy appropriate clothes for myself, and now she's telling me that she won't buy them for me either.

How can I be in this predicament at the age of thirty? I feel like a child, dependent on my mother for something absolutely fundamental.

And now Mum's provision of this basic need has become dependent on me complying with her expectations.

I am forty-four years old.

My doctor has referred me to Valerie, a therapist and dietician who specialises in working with people with eating disorders.

In one of our first few sessions, I outline my long history of struggle with my weight and my relationship with my body and food. We are discussing how I feel when I am told, directly or indirectly, to limit what I eat.

Valerie asks, 'If you were to put words on the feeling of being told not to eat so much, what would you say?'

My response is instant: 'Don't you dare deprive me!' I snap angrily.

'"Deprivation" is a very strong word,' Valerie observes. 'Who is depriving you?'

'My mother,' I reply, without even needing to think about it.

'Tell me about your mother's view of your relationship with food,' Valerie invites.

'Well, I've always known that my body is unacceptable to my mother,' I reply. 'No matter what size I am, or how much weight I lose, I know I will never be what she wants me to be. I've felt the feeling of being unacceptable to her, deep in my bones, from the time I was a young child. Whenever I've lost weight over the years, it's never been enough for her. And when I eat in front of her, I always feel her disapproval – like she's always thinking I'm eating too much, no matter what and how much I eat.

'I sometimes think that if I could stay alive without eating at all, then she would want me to do just that … to just stop eating altogether – forever.'

'It sounds like you think her solution is for you to be permanently "deprived" of something absolutely fundamental to your survival?'

'Exactly!' I say. 'She's been giving me news articles about people who've lost massive amounts of weight through gastric banding for years now. I'm sure she really thinks that if I could just stop eating, the problem would be fixed.

'But I can't even imagine what it would feel like to have a gastric band inside me, stopping me from eating whenever I need or want to, even making me feel sick when I'm just hungry. Depriving me of the most basic thing I need to survive … and of any enjoyment I might have in eating the things I love!'

'No wonder you don't want to consider weight loss surgery,' Valerie says. 'It would almost be like having your mother surgically implanted in your stomach.'

- Three -

Etched in My Skin

My mind works hard to shun the pain
But my body bears it all

Heavy Load

A hundred thousand memories
Are held within my bones
The screams too hard to utter
Ring out in flesh and blood

My story has been scribbled
In the parchment of my skin
My frame, a silent witness
To the terror choked before

My mind works hard to shun the pain
But my body bears it all

And it's a heavy load to carry
A heavy load to bear
A heavy load to live with
A load of pain and fear
It's a heavy load to move with
So heavy to endure
A load that never lightens
Ever-present, always here

My back, it bears the burden
Of the grief that weighs me down
As yesterday's remnants
Still stain beneath the tears

My mind works hard to shun the shame
But my body bears it all

It's a heavy load …

Words © Monique Lisbon 2020
Music © Adrian Hannan 2020

School holidays come and Mum is driving my brother Grant and me to a tennis camp in Phillip Island. I have never been on one of these camps before. Grant has, and he told me that there's an awards ceremony at the end of each camp. Last time, the 'Overall best tennis player' got a new tennis racquet. And the person who won the 'Most improved' award got a sportsbag!

I would *love* to win a sportsbag. Given the fact that I've barely played tennis, I know I'm not very good at it ... so maybe it would be possible to improve enough during the week to win 'Most improved'?

I am thirteen years old.

When we arrive at the camp, we meet all the other kids. Grant knows some of them from previous camps, but everyone is a stranger to me. I introduce myself to the others and choose a bunk bed in the girls' dormitory, then put my suitcase in the locker room.

'How long have you been playing tennis?' asks Maddie, one of the other campers.

'I've never really played before, so I'm really not very good,' I admit. She invites me to have a hit on the tennis court anyway. The official camp program is not starting until tomorrow, so we're free just to settle in and muck around on the courts until then.

I am nervous, and excited. I pull on my brand new white runners and grab my racquet – a second-hand one I inherited from Grant after he got a new racquet for Christmas.

Maddie and I make our way out to the courts, and start hitting the ball back and forth. I miss the ball a lot of the time and, although I'm embarrassed at being so hopeless at tennis, I can also laugh at myself. Maddie laughs too. It's quite fun!

After about twenty minutes, I find that I'm actually able to hit some balls back. As long as I keep my eye on the ball, right up until it hits the strings on the racquet, and then keep watching it even after I've hit it, I seem to be able to get it back over the net. Maybe I'm not as bad at this as I thought.

'Let's play an actual game,' Maddie says, and she takes her position to serve the ball.

Maddie wins the first game hands-down. I don't even score a single point. But it doesn't matter – I'm involved and I'm happy.

Then it's my turn to serve. The first ball I serve lands in the right part of the court, and Maddie hits it back … right into the net!

'Fifteen-love … that's in your favour!' she says.

I've just won my first ever point in tennis, and I'm very excited! Maddie is excited for me too!

Wow! This is so great!

Just then, Grant walks past the tennis court. I look up at him, beaming proudly – did he see me win that last point?

'Kneel!' Grant orders, and my heart sinks.

Before we left for camp this morning, Grant challenged me to a bet. If I won, he said he would give me his dessert at tennis camp for the next two days. And if he won, then his reward was that he could tell me to 'kneel' at any time over the next two days, and I would have to drop whatever I'm doing and kneel down on the ground, then and there.

He won the bet.

So now, when he walks past the tennis court and claims his prize, there is nothing I can do to resist.

Maddie watches in silent puzzlement, as I drop to my knees, then and there, on the tennis court, until Grant finishes walking by, laughing.

When he is out of sight, I scramble to my feet, but avoid looking Maddie in the eye.

We finish the game, mostly in silence.

I don't score any more points.

And at the end of the week, someone else wins the sportsbag.

Summer arrives, and Grant and I are back at Phillip Island.

I am fourteen years old.

During the last year, I went to Weight Watchers and lost 13 pounds. Back at the tennis camp, I see some of the kids who were here last year, including Maddie, and they congratulate me on my weight loss.

There's a new tennis coach this year called Anthony. He is about twenty-five years old and seriously good-looking. Anthony overhears Maddie complimenting me and, when we're alone together in the bushland behind the tennis courts, he asks me how I lost the weight.

I tell him that I went on a diet and reached my goal weight at Weight Watchers during the year. Maybe this will make me better at tennis?

Anthony says to me, 'Well, it's really good that when you lost the weight, you didn't lose your curves.'

I blush. I have only just started wearing a bra a month ago, and I haven't yet got my period – but I know that won't be far away either. I like feeling more like a 'woman', but it is a bit embarrassing when a cute guy like Anthony points out that my body is developing.

Anthony suggests that he could give me some special lessons, just the two of us, to help my tennis skills develop. I am determined to win the 'Most improved' prize this year, and I'm flattered that Anthony would want to spend time with me on my own, so I agree.

The tennis coaches don't stay in the dormitories like the kids – they have their own rooms in a separate part of the campsite – rooms with normal beds, not bunk-beds.

My special lessons happen in Anthony's room, not on the tennis court. They are at night after the other kids are asleep in the dorm. When he takes off my pyjamas, lies on top of me on his bed, and puts his hands all over my 'curves', he says it's a kind of weight-bearing exercise that will help my body get stronger. You need a strong body to play tennis well. I am confused and afraid. I feel like I'm doing the wrong thing, but he's good-looking, and he seems to like me. He is also the coach; he must know what he's doing. So, I don't do anything to stop him.

On day three of the camp, my period finally arrives. When I realise what's happening, I'm not sure what to do as I don't have any sanitary pads with me. I finally tell Corinne, one of the women coaches, and she fixes me up with supplies.

From that point on, Anthony doesn't want to help me with the weight-bearing exercises at night anymore. He says it's too messy. I am relieved to not have him lie on top of me and 'feel my curves' anymore, while I feel ashamed that I let him touch my naked body in the first place.

At the end of the week, at the awards ceremony, I don't win the 'Most improved' award. I do win the award for the 'Hardest trier'. My prize is a tin of tennis balls. I am pleased, yet I feel guilty because I think I've cheated – maybe the only reason I won was because of my 'extra lessons' with Anthony?

Mum comes to pick Grant and me up from the tennis camp, and asks how the week went. When we're on our own together, I tell her I had special lessons with Anthony the tennis coach, and also that I got my period while I was away.

'Oh dear, I was afraid that might happen,' she says.

I'm not sure if she is referring to me getting my first period, or whether she has somehow worked out what Anthony and I were doing during the special lessons.

She gives me a packet of sanitary pads to keep in my drawer for next time.

And I don't breathe another word about the special weight-bearing lessons.

I am twenty years old.

Living in Jason's house is the closest thing to a 'safe place' I've ever experienced. I love my big bedroom there, and Jason has let me move my piano from my parents' house to his lounge room.

Jason is also incredibly supportive of me emotionally, often staying up late at night to listen to me talk about the emotional roller-coaster I seem unable to get off.

I am currently on sick leave from work, and I have deferred my university studies. I don't often leave the house, as I feel intensely uncomfortable even going to the nearby supermarket for fifteen minutes – sometimes that's enough to cause me to have a panic attack.

I am sitting on my bed, and have just got off the phone from a close friend. Rebecca says that she is busy studying for exams, and doesn't have time to come and visit me this weekend.

Even though I'm not studying at the moment, I do remember how stressful exam time is. I understand why Rebecca can't come and see me. But does she know how desperate and alone I feel, and how much it helps to have friends come and be with me when I can't leave the house?

I feel ashamed. I know that I'm being unreasonable in expecting Rebecca to drop everything, yet knowing that I'm being unreasonable doesn't help me put aside my hurt and shame – it just increases it. I feel powerless and helpless in the face of my intense distress.

I start crying, and the tears soon escalate into loud sobs. Then my body starts to shake violently. Before long, I find myself in the middle of a full-blown panic attack. I start screaming, and my friend Janette runs in from the lounge-room where she's been sitting and talking with Jason.

When Janette bursts through the door, she sees my arms flailing around and my whole body convulsing. Janette grabs my arms and tries to settle me by holding them forcibly by my side. This only makes it worse. I feel trapped by her tight grip. The helplessness I felt about my inability to control my intense emotions a few minutes ago, has now turned into a physical powerlessness.

'Help me, help me, *help me*!! I can't, I can't, I can't, I can't …', I sob.

Janette replies, 'What can't you do, Mono? What can't you do?'

But there's no way I can explain.

Jason enters the room, and carefully pries Janette's hands from my arms. Then he sits next to me and holds me, rocking me back and forth.

'You don't have to do anything, Mono,' he says. 'You're OK, you don't have to do a single thing.'

Released from the pressure of expectation, as well as from the feeling of being physically trapped, I soon settle in Jason's arms, and my screams decrease to small baby's whimpers, eventually stopping altogether.

I am twenty-two years old.

I have recently been spending time with Richard, a new friend who I've been writing songs with. Richard and I have gone out for coffee with a friend of his, Alex.

It's 8pm and we are at a trendy café in Fitzroy, surrounded by heaps of attractive and arty people. Alex and I need to sit quite close together in order to be able to hear each other over the live band.

Alex asks me about my music, and we talk about his poetry. I have already read one of his poems, which Richard set to 'blues' music and played to me recently – a sad poem about Alex's previous relationship breakup, and his broken heart. The words are really good; not overly sentimental, but raw and real. They really work as the lyrics of a 'blues' song.

Alex and I really seem to click, and I find I am really enjoying his company.

I go to the bathroom. When I return to the table, I notice Alex's eyes following my every move as I weave my way through the throngs of people in the crowded café. Since I have recently lost weight, I have been getting used to being more able to manoeuver my body through tight places. But I'm really not used to guys looking at me in the way Alex is looking at me now.

I realise that Alex finds me physically attractive, and I start to get scared.

When we are leaving the café, Alex asks if it's OK if he gives me a call during the week – and he suggests that maybe we could go out to a movie together.

I agree. But I feel intensely uncomfortable. By the time I've driven home, I feel filled with such a strong sense of shame – shame that a guy could find me physically or even sexually attractive – and I know I need to find some way to settle the intense discomfort I am feeling.

It feels like the shame is sitting right there, inside my body, not in my head. It starts to feel painful; unbearable. It's like my body is just screaming with all the shame it is holding.

I know I need to stop the agony by getting rid of this sense of shame somehow – to cut it out of myself. So I pull out a razor blade and carve the word 'BAD' into my chest.

Afterwards, I feel strangely settled, and the sense of shame is gone. I am no longer in pain; I feel like I'm floating far away. I cannot even feel my body anymore.

I fall asleep surrounded by a mass of bloody tissues.

I am thirty-six years old.

For the last month or so, I have been reliving memories of abuse by my father; trapped in his car, after my mother drove off and left us there together.

I feel unable to find any kind of resolution for this memory, and it repeats over and over in my mind. It repeats when I'm awake and when I sleep. I feel as though I am still trapped inside that car from thirty years ago.

Everything spirals. I take an overdose and wind up back in a hospital emergency room for the first time in over a decade.

I try to distract myself by meeting a friend for dinner in Acland Street, St Kilda. I drive to the restaurant but cannot find a carpark nearby. Being a Saturday night, the trendy suburb is packed with people.

Eventually I find a spot about 400 metres away. I park the car and begin walking to the restaurant. Quickly, I start to feel an unbearable pain in my feet. I feel like I am walking on hot coals, my skin seared with every step.

This is not the first time this has happened, but it is the worst it's been. It takes me forty minutes to hobble the 400 metres to the

Inch by Inch

restaurant, and I get there half an hour late in complete agony.

In the following weeks, I attend a number of appointments with medical specialists; all trying to get to the bottom of this strange and painful symptom. One test involves having electric pulses projected into my feet and, though the sensation itself is not painful, I become very distressed with the thought of being electrocuted.

None of the tests turns up any results, and the specialists are left puzzled.

My therapist Sandra suggests that the issue, whilst having a very clear physical manifestation, might stem from a psychological cause. She refers to it as 'somatoform dissociation'[6], a way in which one's body carries and expresses traumatic memory physically.

It's like the pain from my trauma needs to be carried and expressed somewhere. When I block it out from my mind, or dissociate it, the only place for it to shift to is my body.

But when I can hold it in my mind, it shifts from my body into a place where I can consciously process it.

Over time, as Sandra and I talk through my traumatic memories and my feelings of being trapped, the emotional pain shifts from feeling utterly excruciating to painful, then just slightly uncomfortable, and eventually almost imperceptible.

As I consciously process the memories in therapy, the painful sensations in my feet start to disappear also.

And before too long, I can walk longer and longer distances without any pain in my feet at all.

---

[6] 'The descriptor "somatoform" indicates that the physical symptoms resemble, but cannot be explained by, a medical symptom or the direct effects of a substance. In the term "somatoform dissociation," "dissociation" describes the existence of a disruption of the normal integrative mental functions. Thus "somatoform dissociation" denotes phenomena that are manifestations of a lack of integration of somatoform experiences, reactions, and functions.' See Ellert R.S. Nijenhuis PhD (2001), 'Somatoform Dissociation: Major Symptoms of Dissociative Disorders' in *Journal of Trauma & Dissociation*, 1:4, 7-32, DOI: 10.1300/J229v01n04_02

- Four -

Escaping My Skin

And I end up sayin'
Goodbye to myself
To save myself

Goodbye to Myself

Woke up this mornin'
Nothin' but dust upon my shelf
Woke up this mornin'
Nothin' to feed myself

Easy to say to ask for help
If you think there's somethin'
There worth helpin'
Not so easy to ask for help
When that somethin' is you
And you loathe yourself

Mornin' on mornin'
My baby moans for mornin' food
Moanin' on moanin'
Screamin' as hard as she could

Somethin' inside her cries for help
She sure must know I got nothin' to give her
Fool to trust me to ask for help
So empty inside
Shame eats my soul

I end up givin'
And I end up taken
A lot and a little
A little and a lot
I end up payin'
And I end up sayin'
Goodbye to myself

So easy to ask for help
If you think there's somethin'
There worth helpin'
Not so easy to ask for help
When that somethin' is me
And I loathe myself

I end up givin' …

To save myself

Words and Music © Monique Lisbon 2008

Inch by Inch

Sunday at 6.30pm finds me making my way to church, just as I've done every weekend for the last two years.

My housemate Jason is leading the service and my close friend Ron is standing up the front, reading the Bible from the pulpit.

I know I belong here. These people are closer than my family and this well-known space is like my second home …

In fact, I would go so far as to say that this is the safest place on earth.

I am twenty years old.

As I listen to Ron's familiar, articulate voice projected through the microphone, my eyes look up at the expansive spread behind the pulpit. The sun is just about to set, and an evocative light is cast through the stained glass windows, forming a vibrant and colourful backdrop to the preacher's platform.

Inside the stained glass window, a Madonna figure holds a small child tenderly in her arms, and other children gather at her feet.

Suddenly, right in front of my eyes, the mother raises her arms high above her head and casts the child to the ground with such force that the whole stained glass window shatters in pieces behind and around Ron and Jason.

I scream and jump to my feet, pushing past the others in my church pew and noisily tearing out of the church in terror.

I run down the stairs to the lower hall, near the function room and entertaining space, and curl up in a ball in the corner of the room. I am hiding behind a row of chairs, not easily seen by Janette, who has followed me from the church in concern. She soon hears me whimpering like a frightened toddler.

'It's OK,' Janette soothes. 'You'll be OK. Do you want to come on out from behind there?'

I feel as though the mother in the window just cast *me* to the ground. I am sweating profusely and my heart is beating like I've run a marathon.

I feel utterly shattered, and any sense of my sanity lies around me in shards.

Did that really just happen? Could I possibly have just imagined it? It was so real, so vibrant. And so scary.

'I just need to be on my own,' I say to Janette.

'OK,' she says, but I can see that she is worried about leaving me alone.

She hesitates, then says, 'I'll just be upstairs in the church. Come and get me if you need me.'

And she is gone.

Even though I asked Janette to leave, now that I find myself on my own, I feel enveloped by an overwhelming sense of panic, fear and abandonment.

The last place I want to be right now is inside my body. I feel like my chest is about to explode. My head is pounding and I feel like throwing up. When I look down at my bare arms inside my summer T-shirt, the wide stretches of skin scream at me like a foreign and decaying mass, ready to pollute me, to swallow me up. There is no chance of escape.

I need to get away from this expansive terror somehow … from my arms … from this danger … from the fear … from my body!

I scramble to my feet and stagger into the kitchen. Opening a drawer, I find a source of escape from all that is locking the terror inside me.

As the knife-blade pierces my skin, I feel an odd, but by now, a familiar sense of relief. Red trails flow thickly and slowly down my arms, breaking up and obscuring the terrifying expanses of danger.

I am no longer here.

I am free.

It is a cold and rainy day. I wish I could just stay in bed, warm and toasty. The last place I want to be is outside in this weather.

Inch by Inch

And the last thing I want to do this day – actually, any day – is be surrounded by scores of people and flashing cameras.

I have no choice. My brother Grant is marrying Margaret today, and she has asked me to be one of her bridesmaids.

I am twenty-one years old.

I have recently come out of a psychiatric hospital after a long, four-month admission. I can still barely go to the supermarket without having a panic attack.

During these last four months, I've been on so much medication to try to curb my anxiety and depression that I regularly sleep up to sixteen or eighteen hours a day. Now that I've been discharged, I am allowed to drive again. Yet every car trip, when I stop at the traffic lights, my eyelids quickly feel so heavy that I fall asleep within seconds and need to be prompted by the horn of the car behind me to set off again.

I was honoured to be asked to be a bridesmaid, alongside the three others – Margaret's sister Dorothy and two of Margaret's university friends. But the other three bridesmaids are all a very different shape from me. Margaret has chosen an olive green satin material for our handmade dresses, and the other three women all look like models; the smooth material flowing down their svelte bodies in a flattering and stylish way.

In contrast, satin does not flatter me. It clings to every bump of my body, of which there are now many. During my recent hospital admission, one of the only things to ward off my despair – and the boredom – was food: chocolate and chips from the vending machine, and crackers and cheese in ready supply from the ward kitchenette. The large doses of medication I've been taking have also contributed to a significant weight gain. After several months of living like this, I no longer fit into the clothes I wore when I was first admitted to hospital, and my body has ballooned to an unprecedented size.

I drag myself out of bed and drive to Margaret's parents' house by 9am to get ready for the wedding. I have brought stockings with me, opaque black ones, which I ordered in advance specially for the occasion, since ordinary stockings from 'normal' shops no longer fit me.

As we are dressing, Dorothy sees me pull out my stockings and start to put them on.

'Oh no,' she says. 'We're all wearing dark grey stockings, not black. And our stockings are much more sheer than those. Yours need to match.'

I start to protest, but she says, 'Don't worry, we bought you a pair too.'

She gives me my pair of sheer dark grey stockings, size XXL.

My heart sinks. I feel too embarrassed to tell Dorothy that there is no way my legs will fit into even XXL stockings if they're from a 'normal' range of stockings, not specialist ones.

Reluctantly, and with a great sense of shame, I sit down to pull on the stockings. They rip near the crotch under my dress, but I do not tell Dorothy. Rather, I say to her, 'I usually wear a second pair of underpants over the top of stockings to help keep them up. I didn't bring a second pair with me today.'

I am hoping against hope that she will realise my discomfort and grant me the licence to wear my opaque black stockings instead. I feel too ashamed to request this directly.

'That's OK, I'll give you a pair of my underpants to wear over the top of the stockings,' Dorothy offers and heads to her bedroom.

For the rest of the day, and right through the evening, I repeatedly try to surreptitiously pull up the underpants – or overpants – over the stockings. The hole in the stockings at my crotch grows larger and larger, cutting ever deeper into the top of my thighs. The overpants keep rolling down over my big belly. There is no way I can keep either the stockings or the overpants up naturally. I feel constantly scared of others noticing my awkward manoeuvers to try to accommodate this untenable situation, or of the whole kit-and-caboodle falling down at my ankles.

After the church ceremony, we travel across town to the reception centre, where the bridal party poses for photos, along with Margaret's and my extended families.

The photographer places each of us like puppets as he wants us, to best set off the scenes he is trying to create. I perch on a chair with my father standing behind me, and the photographer directs my father to place his hand on my back.

The last four months in hospital have been filled with therapy sessions of me talking about my fear of my father, and starting to tell details of the sexual abuse he subjected me to for years as a child. Now it is absolutely excruciating to feel the hand of my father, my perpetrator, on my back, all the while fully expecting my pants to fall down at any second.

'One two three ... smile!' says the photographer. I stifle a scream, instead forcing out the word 'cheese' through my clenched grimace.

When we get into the large reception room, family friends and acquaintances bustle around, making small talk. I am asked repeatedly what I am doing these days. I feel too ashamed to say that I haven't been able to work or study all year because I have been in a psychiatric hospital for months.

I repeatedly escape to the bathroom, to pull up my stockings, touch up my lipstick, try to wipe away the tears without blurring my mascara, and to refreeze the smile on my face.

Back in the reception room, I escape from the socialising and dancing – and the shame – by returning again ... and again ... and again ... and again ... to the buffet table.

I am thirty-three years old.

I've spent much of the last thirteen years in a 'revolving door' scenario, trying to find a sense of safety and a way forward within the walls of psychiatric hospitals.

At the end of last year, my psychiatrist Dr Daniel called an end to our therapy as he recognised that it was no longer helping me. I was stuck. Whilst I was initially extremely resistant to this perceived abandonment by Dr Daniel, I was then very grateful to find and see a specialist trauma therapist, Philip, for the next nine months.

I have worked hard with Philip. He has helped me see that my ongoing issues are the understandable results of trauma, not expressions of an underlying, arbitrary 'illness' that is beyond my or anyone else's control. As we've started to look at, tease apart, and address the issues that kept me stuck for so long, I have moved and changed at an unprecedented pace.

Now Philip has retired after many decades of working with trauma survivors, bringing our therapy to an abrupt end.

In the weeks after my final session with Philip, I feel determined to 'prove' to him *in absentia* – as well as to the world and myself – that my work with him was successful; that I no longer need therapy, and that I have changed and healed beyond recognition.

I have started a new computer business and am trying to build up a client base and source of regular income, in the face of significant computer hardware issues that I cannot afford to fix. Out of inexperience, I have significantly underquoted for a large job for a new client. I am now labouring around the clock to try to complete my obligations using faulty technology, having already been paid in full for the work.

For several months after I finish seeing Philip, I survive on just a few hours' sleep per night, spending much of the rest of the time working, but never seeming to come up for air or find a way forward financially. My 'to do' list is always longer at the end of the day than the start.

My friends and acquaintances are stunned by my very different presentation of being. Those who have known me for some time, cannot believe that I am regularly sleeping only a few hours per night; having seen me, at the peak of my depression, barely able to stay out of bed for more than six or eight hours a day. Those who have witnessed me in my 'stuck' state for so long while I was seeing Dr Daniel, and who have visited me through the many revolving door hospital admissions, now see someone who can't stop moving.

No longer sedentary, I am now running for my life.

In my frenzied state, as well as often forgetting to sleep, I also regularly forget to go to the toilet or to eat. A full day can easily pass by without me remembering to tend to either of these basic bodily needs.

And the weight soon begins to fall off me. Over the course of just a few months, I lose around 30kg.

A few friends are taken aback at the new extremes they are witnessing in me. They recognise that the changes are not coming from a healthy place, and some of them encourage me to find another therapist to keep working on the issues I am determined to deny still exist.

My housemate Heather uses humour to express her concern. She prints a cartoon for me, depicting a mouse working away at the computer in the wee hours of the morning. Another mouse appears in its pyjamas at the darkened door, holding a sign saying 'www.go-to-bed.com'.

I laugh and stick the cartoon above my computer desk. But I continue to ignore its sage advice night after night.

Unlike Heather, the bulk of my friends actually affirm this 'new' me – one who they see as proactive, energetic and upbeat. I am finally losing the weight that has been problematic for so long, and when I bump into people I haven't seen for some time, they no longer recognise me – so great are the changes in my physical appearance, and even more so in my whole demeanour.

Having come from over a decade of feeling I simply *can't* do so many things, I have now embraced a *can do* attitude that I am determined to maintain.

I *can* function without sleep.

I *can* function without food.

I *can* function in, and build up, a business – even without basic working tools.

In fact, I *can* function in ways that ordinary people can't.

My adrenalin, momentum and denial enable me to maintain my newfound way of being for quite a few months.

But eventually, both my mind and body give way and I crash in a physical and emotional heap.

As I grind to a halt, the numbers on the scales start climbing up again. Ultimately I stop looking at them altogether.

- Five -

Stuck

And even if I could move
This prison is my only home

Solitary Confinement

Every cell inside me
Is trapped inside this cell called 'me'
This world that holds me captive
Is chained in skin and bone

An open door stands taunting
A mirage of another world
Every wisp of freedom
Mocks who I've become

And even if I could move
This prison is my only home
And even if I could leave
How could I ever flee myself?

Solitary confinement
I live within a five-foot cell
Solitary confinement
It's hostile and it's home
Solitary confinement
Lying crippled by a rock-hard wall
Solitary confinement
Trapped, forever and alone

And even if I could stand
There's nowhere that I could go
And even if I could see
How could I ever find the way?

Solitary confinement ...

Words © Monique Lisbon 2020
Music © Adrian Hannan 2020

If I were allowed to do three extra Maths or English classes every week, instead of Sports classes, I would be so relieved.

Even Geography or History would be better than this.

I am fifteen years old.

It's not just that I dislike Sports – it's that it is the one place at school where I feel totally and utterly hopeless, with no way to overcome it. This kind of work is far harder than the work I do in any of my other classes.

It's Friday at 2.30pm, and the last class for the week is Sports. When will it all be over? I can't wait for the weekend.

I squirm into my sports tunic in the change-room. It is so embarrassing trying to get changed without any of the other girls seeing my body. And these sports tunics are so short. I would never choose to wear skirts this short; so short that everyone can see my hideous flabby legs!

Just outside the sports building, on the steps to the oval, the sports teacher gives us our mission.

'Now I want you to run around the perimeter of the school,' she says. 'No cutting across the middle of ovals – make sure you stay right around the edges. And run around *all* of the buildings.'

She points to several buildings down the hill where the junior school is. I can't even see what's beyond them; the grounds are so extensive and sprawling.

'You've got thirty-five minutes. That should give you enough time to get all of the way around the whole school. At 3.15pm, we'll all gather back here on these steps, and go inside in time to get changed and go home.'

We set off. A large group of girls speeds off in haste, chatting and laughing, and others take up a slower jogging pace in smaller clusters.

Inch by Inch

I start running also, as fast as I can.

But within just a few minutes, there is no-one else near me. Everyone is much faster than me, even those who are only jogging. The distance quickly grows between the nearest group of girls and me.

Before too long I can't see any of the others at all.

I struggle around the edges of the oval, the gardens, the outskirts of the school buildings. My running pace doesn't last long. All alone, I soon slow to a jog and then to a walk.

After about twenty minutes, I realise I am only a third of the way there.

I try to pick up my pace to increase my chances of making it, but this is a lost cause. I simply can't run for more than a minute at a time, then I have to stop to catch my breath and I feel like I'm going to faint because I'm puffing so much.

After forty minutes, I cut across the junior school oval, and miss two of the buildings altogether. I know I'm meant to go all the way around, but I just don't care anymore. And who can see me now anyway?

Eventually, at 3.50pm, I reach my goal – the steps to the oval. No-one is waiting; they have all long gone. Alone, I walk inside and get changed.

Walking up to the main school building, I ring my mother and ask her to come and pick me up.

It's now after 4pm, and Mum asks me why I'm ringing so late.

I don't want to admit that it took me twice as long to run around the school as everyone else, and that I didn't even run all the way around anyway.

So I simply say, 'Sorry, I worked back late in my final class and missed the bus.'

I am forty-six years old.

I love my current job: working part-time as the Administrator and Office Manager of a Christian contemplative spirituality centre.

I love the work, the people, and the whole atmosphere and ethos of the place. I love the trust that is placed in me, and the absence of micro-managing by those I am answerable to. And I love the flexibility I am given to work the hours I want, as long as everything gets done.

I live just 2km from the centre, and drive there each day, parking my car just a few metres from the main door in an all-day parking spot.

It's all very convenient, and really couldn't be easier.

Occasionally my colleagues and I have work lunches up the street at a local café, to celebrate each other's birthdays. It's only a five-minute walk to the local haunts, but when I know that a lunch is planned, I always set my work hours for that day to begin in the afternoon. That way, I can meet the others at the café before I start work. I make sure I park in a one-hour zone on the main street, right outside the café. This means I have a legitimate reason to drive my car the 300 metres to the all-day carpark and my office main door.

Currently I am the heaviest I've been in my life, so walking even 300 metres while carrying a 200kg load is no mean feat.

One of my regular tasks is to pick up the mail from the nearby post office. The post office is also only a few minutes' walk from the centre, but I always make sure I pick up the mail on the way to work. If I were to drive to work and then have to walk even five minutes up the street to get the mail, I'm not sure I would be able to manage it.

All of this is done without explanation or justification to my colleagues. I try to do it in a way that no-one will even notice. In my head, ahead of time, I'm forever working out ways around potential scenarios, before I find myself caught in an embarrassing situation where I have to move … and can't.

It's Wednesday evening and I am staying back late at work. My car is in its all-day parking spot and I have started my workday midway through the afternoon. I am at an evening workshop at the centre, and my role is to introduce the guest facilitator and generally make the participants feel welcome.

Everyone helps themselves to tea and coffee, and the workshop runs smoothly. Conversation flows naturally afterwards, and then the participants and facilitator leave, one by one.

Finally, I am left alone in the centre. The room is a mess, with chairs having been moved out of place and empty coffee cups sitting at odd intervals.

I look at the room in dismay. It takes me ten minutes to move the chairs back into place and to gather up the empty coffee cups. In that short time, all my energy is spent. I am utterly exhausted, and feel like collapsing physically.

I finish cleaning up the room, switch off the lights, lock the doors and prepare to carry the tray of coffee cups up the six steep stairs to the kitchen.

Mustering all my strength, I struggle up just two stairs. I have to stop as my legs feel like they are about to give way under me. I dare not sit down on the steps, as I'm not sure I'll be able to get up again.

It takes me several minutes to carry the coffee cups up the six stairs. I am puffing and panting like I've run a marathon, and my face is bright red. I can feel sweat dripping down my face.

I place the cups in the dishwasher and sigh with relief.

I have done what I need to do, and can now stagger to my car, just ten metres away, and drive home.

As I close the door behind me, I feel a knot in the pit of my stomach as I realise I have forgotten to put the milk in the fridge.

The mere thought of going back inside, fetching the milk from downstairs, struggling back up the six stairs, and putting it in the fridge, fills me with dread. It is utterly beyond me.

I drop my body into the carseat, so physically exhausted that I can barely bring myself to turn the key in the ignition.

At that moment, the feeling of being trapped hits me like never before. My body feels like a prison. There is simply no escape. I can dress up the prison in my mind, pretending to myself that it's set up oh-so-comfortably, just the way I want it, and that I am not impacted by its constraints. But in reality, I am utterly confined by my lack of choice and power over the most basic of things.

I start crying, and simply can't stop.

And I'm not just crying over the milk.

I am forty-seven years old.

Jodi is one of my oldest friends. We went to university together and shared a student house together in our early twenties. Now that Jodi lives interstate, I only get to see her once or twice a year, when she comes to visit for a holiday.

We've just spent a wonderful couple of weeks together. We've been out to dinner and for drives to the country, and watched movies together. Jodi has done odd jobs around my house, and cooked wonderful meals for the two of us. We've sat and talked for hours on end, and listened to music together.

Now the time has come for Jodi to fly home. The airport is about forty minutes' drive away, and I've set my alarm to ensure I get up to drive her there in time for her early morning flight.

Jodi is gathering her bags together, ready to put into the car.

I have just had a shower and am in my room getting dressed. I perch on the edge of my bed with just a bra and underpants on, and lean over to try to pull on my socks.

I find it hard to reach my feet, even sitting on the edge of the bed, and fall to the floor.

Jodi hears the loud thud as I fall, and runs in to see if I'm OK.

I am not hurt. I simply cannot move. I am sitting on the floor at the foot of the bed, one sock on and one sock off.

I am stuck.

I appeal to Jodi for help – but she is about a third of my size, and there is no way she can help to lift me up.

'Can't you lean on the bed and pull yourself up that way?' she suggests.

I try, but it doesn't work. I can't roll over onto my knees and, without doing that, I can't get the right angle to pull myself up against the bed.

'Maybe you could ring a tall male friend who could lift you up?'

Jodi says.

I feel humiliated and ashamed. I am sitting half-naked on the floor, and am far too embarrassed to call anyone at all.

'Mono, what are we going to do?' Jodi says. 'My flight leaves soon – I really need to go. I'm really sorry …'

'It's not your fault, Jodi,' I reply. I tell her where to find my wallet. Thankfully there is a $100 note there, which I give to her. Then I ask Jodi to fetch the phone, which is out of my reach, and I call a taxi for her.

I say, 'Just leave the front door unlocked when you leave. And please get me my nightie to put back on, so at least I'm decent!'

'What are you going to do, Mono?' she asks, and I reply, 'Don't worry – I'll work it out somehow.'

'I'm so sorry,' she says again. 'I love you.'

Jodi bends down to give me a hug on the floor and I look at her with a mixture of amusement, frustration and despair.

As I watch, she effortlessly picks herself up and glides through the house with her luggage to wait outside the front door for the taxi.

I hear the taxi pull off outside the house.

Then I pick up the phone next to me.

'Triple-0. What is your emergency?' A woman's voice parrots the well-worn phrase through the headset.

Embarrassed, I mutter my response under my breath.

I must be the only forty-seven year old in the history of the world who needs an ambulance to help her get up off the floor.

'You know, it's just a construct of our superficial, misogynistic, consumeristic, looks-obsessed society that makes people – particularly women – feel bad about weighing more than a certain arbitrary number of kilograms,' Amanda says. 'Nothing else. There's actually nothing wrong with being the size you are, objectively speaking.'

I nod. I understand what Amanda is saying, and I agree – to a certain degree.

I am forty-eight years old.

It's been over twenty years since Amanda and I have seen each other, so I imagine that she must find it confronting to see how much weight I've gained during that time, even if she denies it. I'm now nearly twice the size I was when I last saw her. I am aware that Amanda is probably trying to reframe the changes in an effort to reassure me that she doesn't judge me for my weight gain, and I really appreciate her efforts.

Amanda and I were friends at university, and studied Philosophy together as part of our Arts degrees. One of the subjects we had both appreciated was Philosophy of Feminism.

'It is still pretty constraining for me to be this size, though,' I say. 'And I wish I could do something about it.'

Amanda says, 'Monique, don't give in to the lies! What does it matter if you wear size 12 or size 14 clothes? That's all just superficial bullshit! Being vain about your looks makes no difference to who you are on the inside. And who has the right to determine what 'normal' is, anyway?'

I smile. I can't even remember the last time I could fit into size 14 clothes. Most of the clothes in my current wardrobe go up to size 28.

I pull out my phone and look at a list I wrote four years ago. When I started seeing Valerie for help with addressing the issues behind my eating disorder, she suggested I write a list of goals for weight loss – the things that might motivate me to lose weight and that I would feel were real achievements.

As I read through the list now, it occurs to me that there is nothing superficial about any of my goals. There is no hint of vanity or giving into social bias.

Every single one of the items in my list is fundamental to my everyday existence, and to my ability to function at the most basic level in the world:

My Weight Loss Goals

- To be able to put on socks easily
- To be able to clean myself when toileting and not have to use a bidet
- To be able to get up off the couch or a chair easily
- To fit into normal seat-belts in the car
- To fly on a plane without a seat-belt extension or having the armrests up
- To be able to fit into the toilet cubicle in a plane
- To fit into cinema seats and chairs with arms
- To shop in normal clothes shops
- To walk up steps without puffing
- To walk more than 100m without my back hurting
- To be able to cut my toenails

- Six -

In My Shoes

Walk a mile in my shoes
Before you tell me to be free

Walk a Mile

Your words fall like lead balloons
Filled with judgment, feigning freedom
You pounce upon my heart with preying claws
Victim to your expectations

Walk a mile in my shoes
Before you tell me how to be
Walk a mile in my shoes
Before you tell me to be free

Words and Music © Monique Lisbon 2005

This would have to be one of my favourite places in the world. Tranquil and beautiful, a place of profound peace, I can feel the stress lift from my shoulders as soon as I enter the Peninsula Hot Springs.

I've been coming here for years, and I never get sick of it. Today I've come with my friend Sally.

I am forty-two years old.

Sally and I arrive and head straight to the change-rooms. I try to hide in a nook of the room behind a wall, attempting to discreetly ensure minimum visibility as I get changed.

As I contort my body, trying to remove my bra without taking off my blouse first, and then pulling up my bathing suit without revealing any of my body, I comment to Sally: 'You have no idea how many people stare at me, even at the best of times. It's like they've never seen a fat person before.'

Sally nods sympathetically. As a long-term friend, she has witnessed what I have gone through for many years. She turns her head and looks away. I realise that she is doing this to try to extend privacy to me.

Even though Sally has seen me through many of my struggles, I can't help but think she would have no idea what it feels like to wear a swimming outfit in public when you're as large as I am.

So I say, 'You know, if you walked around for just one day in a body the size of mine, you'd realise how many people stare at you, like you're a circus freak. And children are the worst ... adults at least try to hide the fact that they're staring, but so many small children are really astonished, even scared, to see someone my size.'

I continue: 'Prejudice against obese people is the last socially acceptable taboo. If children were to stare at someone, or make a rude comment, just because they're black or gay or had a physical disability, most parents would be very quick to pull them into line. But it's like there's a kind of social contract that permits everyone to show contempt for fat people – so most parents don't say anything if their kids are rude to people who are obese. I sometimes think that people are scared obesity might be contagious, so if their kids dislike fat people, perhaps that will prevent them from catching the terrible affliction!'

Sally laughs uncomfortably. Since we are good friends and I rarely feel judged by her, I assume her awkwardness is a result of her desire for me not to feel too embarrassed. She simply doesn't know what to say.

I quietly pick up my towel and follow Sally outside, trying to avoid the stares of the other people we walk past.

Walking through the world two or three times the size of everyone else means I often sense their discomfort and dislike towards me, even disdain. This is usually subtle and unspoken. But it is deeply palpable.

Sally and I have the first spring to ourselves, and sit together in silence, enjoying the drizzling rain on our faces and warm water on our bodies; soaking in the serene environment.

After about half an hour, we move to the next spring – the cave pool. Sally lies back on the shallow ledge, relaxing in the steamy waters, her head propped up on an inflatable pillow. I sit next to her and soak in the warmth.

A man and his young daughter enter the spring. I can feel the staring eyes of the little girl, about four years old. She does not take her wary eyes off me.

I smile at her father and try to make small talk.

'Perfect day for the springs,' I say to him. He smiles uncomfortably and looks away in embarrassment, grabbing hold of his daughter's shoulders to steer her away from me.

The pair starts to move through the pool towards the cave at the back.

I try again to lighten the mood. 'You be careful in there,' I say to the little girl. 'There might be monsters!'

She giggles shyly but doesn't say anything. She still appears stunned to see someone my size up close.

After the father and daughter have moved out of earshot, I say to Sally, 'Did you notice how scared she was of me? And how embarrassed her father was? It's like they've never seen someone who is obese before.'

We lie back in the water for another ten minutes or so, and then the father and daughter re-emerge from the cave.

'How was it?' I say to the little girl. 'Did you see any monsters?'

'Yes!' she replies.

'Wow!' I say, 'Were they big and scary?'

Without pause, the little girl blurts out, 'Not as big and scary as you!'

Without a word, her father turns his head and looks the other way, ushering his daughter quickly out of the pool.

It's Friday evening and I'm meeting my friend Carly for dinner and a movie.

I am forty-three years old.

My left knee has been feeling the effects of my weight gain for quite some time, and now I find it hard to walk without pain. Reluctantly I've recently bought a walking stick. Using the stick is the only way I can get around without my legs collapsing under me. I couldn't cope with the thought of buying a boring brown walking stick from a mobility aid shop for 'old people', so I ordered a funky multi-coloured stick online. It matches the rainbow colours in my patterned clothes. While I'm often tempted to hide behind black clothes, I try to make a point of buying colourful clothes that are suitable for someone my age.

I may find it hard to walk, but I'm only forty-three years old, not eighty-three!

Carly and I enter the restaurant. There's a bit of a queue for tables, so we take a seat near the entrance.

After the people ahead of us in the queue are seated, I say to the waitress, 'Table for two?'

'Just a minute,' she says, then rushes off to clear a table.

Then she walks back down the two steps to the foyer of the restaurant. 'This way,' she says, smiling at Carly and me.

I put my stick on the ground next to my chair and push myself upright, then begin to follow Carly and the waitress.

As we approach the two stairs, the waitress suddenly reaches out and grabs hold of my arm.

'This way, dear,' she says in a loud sing-song voice, slow and deliberate, as though I'm deaf. 'Careful now, you don't want to fall!'

I look at Carly in astonishment. The waitress must be just twenty years old, so I guess I am old enough to be her mother. But never before have I been made to feel like a grandmother – or even a great-grandmother!

The waitress doesn't remove her hand from my elbow, instead carefully and slowly escorting me to the table like I'm a porcelain doll that might break if she isn't extra-careful.

Carly and I sit down and the waitress leaves. We both burst out laughing.

'Do I actually look like I'm eighty-three?' I say. 'I know my hair is due for a colour soon, but I had no idea the grey hairs were that visible!'

We shake our heads in amazement, and I try to laugh it off.

But it still stings to feel that someone, even a stranger, can't see past the limitations of my failing body to the strong, capable and functional woman inside.

I am forty-four years old.

I have recently had a fall and my left knee is feeling the after-effects. I find it very painful to walk, and standing in the one spot for more than a minute or two is agony.

My general practitioner has sent me to an orthopaedic surgeon for an MRI and further examination.

I wait outside Dr McQuinn's office, and soon he ushers me in.

I try to explain, 'I fell down some stairs a week ago, and my knee has been hurting ever since …' I begin.

Dr McQuinn cuts me off.

'Exactly how much do you weigh?' he asks bluntly.

I am taken aback. There is no subtlety to his question, and he is asking it with all of the tact and concern of a gnat.

I start to justify myself. 'At the moment, I'm about 160kg,' I reply. 'I did lose 40kg, but then put back on 20kg.'

'So you're 20kg up?' he says bluntly.

Angrily, I reply, 'No, I'm 20kg down!'

'Well. What do you expect?' he retorts. 'How do you think your knee can cope carrying that kind of weight?'

I fall silent and blink back tears. Does he really think I'm unaware of how heavy I am? How can I not know it? I carry this load every day of my life.

The burden of his judgment and disdain falls even more heavily on my shoulders. He sends me across the road for an MRI, and I am mortified to find that I cannot even fit into the machine. It is impossible for the tests to be taken.

I get back into my car and drive home, my sight obscured by my tears.

A few weeks later, I summon the courage to ask my doctor for a referral to a different knee specialist. The pain has not subsided and I need to find a way forward.

It takes another month to get in to see Dr Treloar, but from the moment I meet him, I feel the difference in attitude. Dr Treloar looks me in the eye and makes sure I'm seated comfortably before he begins to examine my knee.

While waiting for the appointment in the last few weeks, I managed to find an MRI machine large enough to do the tests. Dr Treloar looks at the results on his screen, and I ask him what he sees.

I am taken aback by his response, so different from that of Dr McQuinn. Unlike Dr McQuinn, it is Dr Treloar's compassion that takes my breath away.

'What I see is so much damage that I actually wonder how you're not walking around screaming,' he says. 'You must be in so much pain, even just standing.'

The validation I feel from this stranger is beyond words.

I nod, then say, 'What can be done?'

'I am not at all an expert in this area,' he says, 'but honestly, the only thing you can do is lose weight. I'm not saying it's easy – and I really have no idea how you're even going to do it, especially when you can barely move. There are others out there who can help you with that much more than I can. But what I do know is that nothing else will help your knee. Surgery won't help because it just won't work. You desperately need a knee replacement, but if I were to give you one, I'd be removing the replacement a month later. Medication will only marginally dull the pain. My heart tells me to book you in to operate on you today, but my head tells me it just won't work. And in the end, I have to listen to my head.

'Basically, the only thing you can do is to lose weight. And it will make a huge difference if you can. I have no idea how you will do it, but it's the only thing that will make a difference.'

I leave Dr Treloar's office feeling a strange mix of despair and hope. I, too, have no idea how I can lose so much weight, but now I realise that I absolutely must. If I don't, I will wind up in a wheelchair, and soon.

I also feel buoyed by the compassion he has shown me. Having someone 'get it' – understand my pain and the feeling of being trapped and unable to move – especially someone in a role that traditionally prioritises hard-nosed pragmatism over heart-felt care – makes the world of difference to me.

When I get home, I call a phone number my general practitioner gave me several months ago. Valerie is a therapist and dietician who specialises in working with people with eating disorders.

I have no idea how, but I know I need to lose weight. And if this medical specialist can show me such respect and compassion, maybe there are other specialists out there who can help me achieve what I need to, with similar care.

I am forty-nine years old.

Over the last year, I have found more specialists to help me with care and compassion than I had ever let myself believe was possible.

I've also worked hard myself. Even with all the support in the world, I could not have achieved what I have achieved in the last year without my own tenacity and sheer effort.

Every week I visit my doctor, Bethany. Within a month or two of beginning to steadily lose weight, I realised that having a set of scales at home was not helping me. Having spent the last two decades avoiding the scales like the plague, I then developed a dependent relationship with them. They helped to keep me on track, while I also felt governed by them, and by my reliance on the numbers they displayed as an indicator of moral vice or virtue.

Eventually, I surrendered my scales to Bethany.

Now I see her weekly for a kind of 'supervised access visit' with my scales. Before I even step on the scales, we talk about how I've been feeling through the week and what effect it will have on me if the numbers don't go in the direction I want. If I'm feeling particularly down on myself, and ready to subject myself to judgment and scorn, then Bethany invites me to choose to not get on the scales that week. Bethany always leaves the choice to me, but she also tries to ensure that I am conscious of what I'm feeling, what I want to do, and why. She extends support and encouragement towards me, unfleetingly, week after week. When there is a blip in my trajectory, she talks with me at length about holding it in the context of the bigger picture. Her compassion towards me teaches me how to be compassionate towards myself.

This morning when I weigh in with Bethany, the scales show an 84kg loss from my highest recorded weight.

I have a cheeky idea, and ring my friend Aaron.

Aaron is a fit and sporty person, over 6 foot tall, but lanky and well-toned. Over the last year, I have increasingly enjoyed talking with him about eating healthily and finding an exercise regime that I enjoy.

Aaron recognises my number and cheerily answers the phone, 'Hi mate. How are you going?'

'Aaron! I've lost you!' I reply.

'What?' he says.

'I've lost you!!' I insist.

'Mono, I have absolutely no idea what you're talking about.'

'Aaron, I've finally and officially lost you!' I say again.

'Mono, what *are* you talking about?' Aaron replies.

I laugh and then explain. 'Well, I weighed in this morning and I've now lost 84kg in total. I was thinking about that, and realised that that's how much you weigh. So I've now officially lost you!'

Aaron's delighted laugh matches mine. 'You are kidding me! That's just amazing!' he exclaims.

His next sentence sums it all up – the difference between the input of people who have judged me for years, and the support of people who have extended compassion and empathy. It's one thing to tell other people what they need to do to change, and another thing entirely to get inside their shoes and understand the obstacles that need to be overcome in order for them to change.

'How the hell did you ever even get out of bed while you were carrying me on your back all those years?'

Compassion makes all the difference in the world.

- Seven -

Skin on Skin

*Now the time has come for me
To make space for my dignity*

Free Rent

You breathe self-awareness from your every pore
The brashness of your shadow draws me to explore
Your naked eyes a beckoning I can't ignore
My guard is down and I fall into you once more

Stranded here, in thirsting dreams, I drown in you
Clinging to the pretence that your pledge is true
As you lie back, am I in your field of view?
'Cos lying seems to come so easily to you

I've been giving you free rent in my brain too long
You have well and truly made yourself at home
But now the time has come for me
To make space for my dignity
There's no more room for you and me
So I'm kicking you out!

You've lured me with your promise of integrity
Then snatched away each morsel of humanity
But now you've broken one too many sacred vows
And so I see right through the lies that you espouse

I've been giving you free rent in my brain too long
You have well and truly made yourself at home
Two is perfect side by side
If one is me and two's my pride
Then three is you, and that's a crowd
I'm kicking you out!

Words © Monique Lisbon 2015
Music © Monique Lisbon and Adrian Hannan 2015

My peers are shifting gears into adulthood and getting married. It seems like every few weeks I receive a least one invitation to celebrate. Most of my friends are conservative Christians, which usually means making the decision to wait until they are married before having sex. The enticement is there to marry sooner than they might otherwise.

I am twenty-one years old.

Invitations all follow a similar pattern, addressed to 'Monique + Friend'. Most of my friends know that there is no-one I would bring along to their functions, while I appreciate their expressed hope that there might be.

It's always interesting to see who I am seated with. The more my friends couple up and marry off, the less single people are left in the mix. Over time, I end up being seated with people I don't know – the great-aunt who has never married, the widowed family-friend, the elderly neighbour.

Through my Christian lens, it would not even occur to me to get sexually involved with anyone outside of marriage. And given that I generally spend a good part of each year in and out of psychiatric hospitals, there's an apparent dearth of interested eligible men.

I am scared to embrace or explore any sexual part of myself. I hate my body and cannot ever imagine it being a source of physical pleasure or positivity. The desire to remain 'pure' as a single Christian provides me with the opportunity to avoid even thinking about this part of myself.

As the months and years pass, the 21st and wedding invitations stop arriving as frequently, replaced with invitations to baby showers and dedications, then 30th and 40th birthday parties, wedding anniversary celebrations, and reunions.

My friends' lives seem to be rapidly changing. My life does not.

By the time I am thirty-five, one notable thing has changed. Whenever an invitation arrives, no '+ Friend' is invited to attend with me.

Having been single for most of my adult life, the topic of sex doesn't often come up in conversation. Generally people assume that either I am not interested or I am 'asexual'.

I am forty years old.

The last two decades have been filled with the struggle to come to terms with the sexual abuse and exploitation I experienced as a child at the hands of several perpetrators. Given what I've been through, it certainly wouldn't be surprising if I weren't at all interested in sex, or if I had shut off that part of myself to such a degree that I could legitimately be called 'asexual'.

Yet the truth is, I *am* interested in sex. I am intensely interested. I just have no opportunity to explore and express it.

I have no idea where to start in finding an appropriate and legitimate context to do so.

One night at 2am, I lie soaked in sweat after waking from an intense dream. In my uncensored nocturnal psyche, I had felt the heady rush and passion of being close to a nameless man. I could move freely, and our bodies danced together in delicious slow motion, winding around the nooks and crannies of each other's most personal space. I felt like I was exploding with joy and freedom.

Now I lie awake, alone and frustrated.

I roll over and grab my laptop which is by my bed. I'm unsure what to search for, but somehow I type the right words into a search engine. Up comes a website called 'Private Guys'. It is not at all seedy – none of the men in the photos are even naked. There are about ten profiles, each with a short bio and photo, and the men all sound, well ... *normal*.

In one of the photos sits a middle-aged man simply named 'Bob'. He is holding a newspaper, and there's a cup of coffee next to him and a dog lying at his feet. He is wearing a T-shirt, jeans and sneakers, and his face is blurred out of recognition.

I do not want to overthink this too much. I want to make a move before I change my mind. I send Bob a text message, asking him to call me back during the day.

I can't believe I actually did that!

I roll over and try to push the thought out of my mind. Maybe when I wake up tomorrow, this will all have been a dream too?

The next morning, I am driving to my therapy session when the phone rings. I do not recognise the number so I assume it may be a new work client.

'Hello, Monique speaking,' I say, donning my usual professional voice.

'Hello, Monique, my name is Bob,' the voice says, equal to mine. 'I'm responding to a message I received. I'm not sure if this is a good time for you?'

I am taken aback. It was clearly not in a dream that I texted Bob.

'Thanks for calling back, Bob,' I say. 'I'm just about to go into a meeting, but I'll call you back after that.'

I hang up, gulp, then go into my 'meeting'. Thankfully, therapy is the kind of meeting where I can talk about this phone call. The session is filled with a discussion about what happened last night, my impulsive decision to search for a sex worker, and what I should do from here.

After an hour of discussing the situation with Sandra, I decide to proceed with meeting Bob.

I end up seeing Bob on and off for ten years. He becomes a very familiar presence in my life. He is entirely present for the hour or two he is there on any given day, and entirely absent for the rest of the time. We get to know each other superficially very well, but I never learn his surname. And whilst he displays an interest in my life on a surface level, I never feel an emotional connection. I do not think about Bob in between bookings or long for anything deeper between us.

Naturally, I do not tell many people about Bob; especially my family or the friends who are still involved in the conservative

Christian world that I inhabited in my twenties. I do not think of this as a 'secret' but rather a 'private' part of my life. I sense that most people would not understand my choice to pay someone for a sexual relationship, and there's a big part of me that also struggles with this.

With the very few friends I do tell about Bob, I jokingly refer to him as 'the longest relationship I've *never* had.'

Bob's parting words are always the same, 'See you next time I'm looking at you.' And it's always up to me when that happens.

Bob affords me the opportunity to get in touch with a positive side of my physical being, my sexuality. One therapist points out to me that what I am paying for is not the sex – it is the safety.

My encounters with Bob are a context for exploring a part of myself that had first been extensively damaged over many years as a child, and then had been long cut off and denied – my sexuality. I find I am able to be present and active sexually in a way I could not be otherwise.

And I start to seek another partner to 'look at me' in this way – someone I will learn to trust to see more than just my body.

I crave connection. I crave much more than what Bob can give me; more than what I pay him for.

I am forty-four years old.

I want to feel that when I cry out from the vulnerable depths of my being, that I am meeting the vulnerable depths of another human being.

I want sex to be about making love, not only about satisfying physical desires.

It's just that when you're my age and you look the size of a house, it's nigh-impossible to find someone willing to look behind the imposing physical façade to the valuable and beautiful tender heart inside.

I know I can't easily find love, real love. So I start looking for the next best thing; the dizzy excitement of instant gratification and physical connection.

The first time I join a sex hookup site, I can't believe what I experience. To date, if I've been daring enough to 'put myself out there' in person, for instance by going to a social gathering with other single people, I've been lucky if even one or two men say 'hello' to me, let alone strike up a longer conversation. I have grown very used to feeling undesirable and unattractive. Who would want to be close to someone like me?

These sites are entirely different.

I'm logged on for less than a minute before there are seven men trying to start up chats with me.

I certainly feel dizzy – dizzy with the headspin of so much attention.

One night, I've been online for twenty minutes, when Vaughan strikes up a chat. He has dark hair and eyes, a thick beard and a stunning smile. Cropped out of the photo is a child on his knee – I can just see the very edge of the toddler's bald head. Vaughan's profile tells me he is doing a Masters in Social Work.

His first words to me are: 'I don't know how you feel about your profile photo, but I can tell you that from my point of view, what you've got makes you totally hot … in a very *big* way.'

Ordinarily that would just sound like a corny pickup line to me. And at one level I know that of course that's all it is. There's no pretence on this site about what we're all there for.

But there's something about Vaughan's photo and words that makes me take notice. Maybe it's the fact that he's holding a toddler on his lap – it looks like he's a father, so he's got some idea of responsibility. Maybe it's the fact that he's studying Social Work – he must have a brain, a conscience and compassion for people, and a desire to make a difference in the world. Maybe it's the fact that he acknowledged in his words that I might have some insecurity about my size, before turning that around to let me know that my size is attractive to him.

Or maybe it's none of those things, and I just choose him because I want to connect with someone … anyone.

Vaughan and I exchange witty and flirtatious chats through the website until finally I give him my mobile number.

We arrange to meet up. Even though he is a stranger and I know it would be wiser and safer to meet him in a public place, I give him my address. We both know what we are intending to do, and we are both looking for the same thing.

Vaughan comes over to my house and we share an intense evening of passion. I had no idea that it was possible for my body to feel so good, so powerful, so alive!

Unlike Bob, I simply cannot get Vaughan out of my mind. We arrange to meet up the following Friday night, and I count down the days.

Friday night arrives, but Vaughan doesn't. I leave multiple messages, frantically thinking that something has happened to him.

After several hours of worry, I receive an email from Vaughan late that evening, with a long explanation about having lost his mobile phone and struggling to buy a new SIM card with the same number. He tells me he is currently borrowing the phone of a kind man on the train to write me this email, and that he has run out of time to come over that night – but he will be in touch soon so we can spend another magic evening together.

I am relieved, and take him at his word.

We see each other a few more times, stolen moments when Vaughan is able to find time away from his co-parenting responsibilities.

Vaughan has told me about his own battle with anorexia, and his tortured relationship with his domineering father. He realised through his own therapy that he saw his only power over his father to be his refusal to eat. In the end, he got better when he came to see that he was only hurting himself, not his father.

I admire Vaughan's self-awareness and his evident hard emotional work to get to a place of being as functional as he is, including helping other people in his role as a rehabilitation support worker.

Undeniably, I have fallen for Vaughan – and I want to believe in the version of him that he has constructed. That version of Vaughan exists in a larger story in which I have a place; a place where I can feel special and alive and connected.

And then.
He stands me up again.
And again.
And again.

Vaughan always has an explanation, so convoluted and in-depth that it's hard to believe someone could invent lie after lie like that. So I keep holding on. Maybe it's better to have 'half a man' than no man at all.

One day, I receive a text from Vaughan out of the blue. He says he misses me and that he'd like to come over and see me that evening. My heart skips a beat.

I am on my way to pick someone up from the airport – a woman from interstate who I am meeting for the first time, and who I will be billeting whenever she comes to Melbourne for a training course.

I tell Rose that I am expecting someone to come over later that evening, a male friend who I've had a bit of involvement with in the past, but haven't seen for a while, and that we'll just stay in my room and talk there, so hopefully we won't disturb her.

After we get home and have been talking for a couple of hours, Rose says to me, 'I really don't know you, so it might be completely out of line for me to say this. Feel free to tell me so and I'll back off.

'I also don't know how you feel about your weight – but I am concerned that you might think that because you are carrying some extra kilograms, that Vaughan is the best you can get. From the little you've told me about him and about things between you in the past – and from what I can see in this intelligent strong woman sitting before me – he's not.'

I am taken aback by Rose's words, but I appreciate her candour.

Vaughan comes over and once again I feel completely smitten.

The next time I hear from Vaughan, it is New Year's Eve. He writes me another text, wanting to hook up. Once again I wait and, of course, he doesn't show up.

A friend tells me, 'Mono, you are giving this guy free rent in your brain. And he doesn't deserve it. Kick him out of there!'

It takes many more conversations with a few people who know me well before I start to hear, and heed, their words.

The clincher comes when a therapist says to me, 'Vaughan is not acting the way he is because of fear. He is not afraid of a relationship. Rather, he is playing with power. He is always putting you in the position where you are beholden to him, waiting on him, grateful to him for any crumbs of attention he gives you. And you know, you're probably not the only woman he's doing it to.'

For some reason, I can finally hear the truth. Perhaps it is because the therapist has explained that he is manipulating me in order to have power over me. I understand the dynamics of power and abuse very well, and am able to recognise that people can exert power in subtle ways. Until that point, I had seen Vaughan's avoidance of a real relationship with me as a result of his fear and insecurity, and I had compassion and patience with him as I knew firsthand that it can take a long time to overcome those issues.

Now I realise that the snippets of truth Vaughan has fed me point to a much larger picture, where Vaughan strives to maintain the upper hand at any cost, even if it means playing on another person's vulnerabilities and insecurities to do so.

Right from the beginning, Vaughan tested out whether my weight was a point of vulnerability and insecurity for me. Then he reframed it so that I felt a false sense of security in him finding that part of me attractive.

I realise that I am placing all of my power, my self-esteem, my hopes for security and purpose and worth, in Vaughan's hands. And his are not trustworthy hands.

So I summon the courage to believe that no man at all is better than half a man.

I take hold of my own dignity, blocking Vaughan's number on my phone, setting up a filter to automatically send his emails to the trash … and kicking him out of my brain.

It takes much longer for me to break the pattern of seeking comfort and solace in the wrong places, and experiencing further damage as a result.

I am forty-four years old.
I am forty-five years old.
I am forty-six years old.

Memories of my initial experience when I hooked up with Vaughan stay with me. It was surreal to find myself with a smorgasbord of men to choose from, and to be met with instant and overwhelming affirmation of my physical being.

I have hated my body for so long, that I can't even imagine what it would feel like to be found physically attractive. Friends often comment on my 'lovely smile', but that has always felt like a backhanded compliment to me. I do trust that they really mean it, but what is most striking to me in this comment is that my smile is the only part of my body they can find to genuinely comment on positively.

I do not tell these friends about trying to find contexts for sexual expression, largely out of shame. I imagine that if I were to even mention that side of myself to anyone, then they would start to imagine me having sex, and that would totally fill everyone with disgust.

I once saw a Woody Allen film in which a man is in bed with a new partner. He is just starting to loosen up and find his way romantically with the woman, when his mother appears by the side of the bed and holds up Olympic scorecards with very low scores.

In my case, my hatred of my body, and my intense sense of shame at being so overweight, is so extreme that I imagine that if anyone close to me saw me naked, even if only in their mind's eye, they would find me utterly disgusting. The scorecard for my physical acceptability would be zero.

It is much easier for me to be naked with a stranger than with someone whose opinion actually matters to me. And it is so tempting to try to overcome my sense of shame and self-disgust at my body with the instant thrill of a sexual fling.

So I return to the sex hookup sites, often late at night, whenever I am feeling vulnerable or alone or looking for a way to escape uncomfortable feelings like grief or shame. It never takes long to find someone willing to step into and fill the void, and I guess many of the men I meet on these sites are looking for someone to fill their own void also. On the odd occasions when a man says he can't meet with me that night, and he suggests meeting the next day instead, I always say 'no'. What I am looking for is a quick fix, the sexual equivalent of fast-food. I also know from experience that by the time tomorrow comes, I will once again be filled with shame and self-loathing for the depths I descended to the night before, and I will unsubscribe myself from the sex sites, vowing never to return.

But I do return, at the next low point in my life, and somehow the logins to the sites still work and the profiles I thought I'd deleted are easily recovered.

I meet many men at these low points in my life. Like eating fast-food, the encounters always over-promise and under-deliver. At some level, I know that I am seeking to feed a deep hunger with empty calories. Just as junk food can't nourish and sustain a person's body, cheap and meaningless sex with a stranger can never satisfy a heart's longing for connection.

Sometimes the damage that is caused is very tangible. On one such occasion, I am raped in my own bed by a stranger. It takes me months to even be able to put the word 'rape' on the encounter, because of the intense shame I feel about getting myself in that situation in the first place. I sought this man out on a sex site, I gave him my address, I took him into my bed, and I lay in his arms afterwards talking about nothing, trying to convince myself that I was OK, that this was all my choice and that I was a mature, enlightened, liberated soul.

Perhaps the greater damage is the long-term reinforcement to myself that I am disgusting and shameful, and that this is the only way anyone could ever stand to be physically close to me.

It takes time … a long time … but eventually the gaps lengthen between my visits to these sites. In those gaps, I increasingly learn to sit with the discomfort of uncomfortable and distressing emotions, rather than trying to flee from them in a transitory fling.

It's now been a few years since I last visited a sex hookup site, and several months since I decided to call an end to my arrangement with Bob.

I am fifty years old.

Having worked hard, both internally and externally, I have lost a significant amount of weight. More importantly, I feel more comfortable in my body, even liking who I am and how I look.

I am pleased to have finally reached a point where I know that I am ready for a real relationship, one in which I can connect emotionally, socially and physically. And I have more of a sense of confidence in myself that I can find good contexts for appropriate kinds of connections.

I join a singles' dinner club, attending dinners with three men and two other women. With only six people present, it's easy to move past superficial conversations, and the fact that there's more than just a couple going on a blind date helps to lessen the pressure and intensity of the situation.

At one dinner I hit it off with Jack, a vocational trainer with several degrees in Educational Psychology. The conversation is enjoyable, and we start seeing each other socially.

I really like Jack. We are on the same wavelength and have interesting conversations about emotional intelligence, social issues, music and business. We visit cafés and go to the movies together.

I am dating in a 'normal' kind of way, with a 'normal' sort of person, for perhaps the first time ever. I am keen to spend more time with Jack to see if we might decide to step up our contact to a deeper relationship.

Jack is quick to tell me that we are not yet in a relationship. Even after several months of seeing each other, he will not agree to come to my house, or to invite me to his. He also has not told his brother, who he lives with, that we are dating. Jack doesn't want things between us to escalate too far physically because 'sex complicates everything.'

We continue to walk the tightrope of spending time together, but not letting things escalate too far or too quickly for Jack's comfort. Over time, I realise that whilst we are on the same wavelength intellectually and psychologically, we are looking for different things in terms of a potential relationship. I am not interested in maintaining a casual interaction that looks like it will stretch on indefinitely without any shift in commitment, and he is not interested in spending more time together to see if he eventually wants to consider having a relationship with me.

After three months, we amicably decide to part ways.

My connection with Ryan is quite different. Meeting at another singles' dinner, I am unsure whether I want to see him again. He talks a lot and doesn't listen a great deal. However, he says a few things during the dinner that earn my respect so, when he says he'd like to see me again, I decide to give it a go.

Ryan is a very fit and active person. As I've lost weight over the last couple of years, I have embraced exercise in an unprecedented way, and have become energised by, even addicted to, physical activity. We share this in common and I love pushing the frontiers of my new body at Ryan's weekend farm by riding on the back of his motorbike and climbing down into a deep ravine to skinny-dip in the secluded chasm below.

Ryan and I spend a lot of time together. He is reliably and solidly there, in a way that Jack simply wasn't. Ryan is present in the relationship, and very early on he expresses a deep loyalty to me.

Yet we are intensely different people, not at all on the same wavelength in terms of religion, politics and several significant social issues. I introduce him to a couple of my friends, but the interactions do not go well. Ryan hates political correctness with a passion, and sometimes says things in order to be provocative.

There are many topics of conversation that we need to simply agree to disagree on, and I find myself avoiding certain topics altogether rather than risk getting an earful of his strong views which are contrary to mine.

I feel that all of this is OK, and that we could get through it all together and learn to co-exist with differing points of view, if only we could communicate openly and honestly. For me, honest and vulnerable communication about emotional matters is central to a relationship. Ryan makes it clear that he is willing to talk about important things only if it is absolutely necessary to do so – and then, it's like getting blood out of a stone.

The key sticking point is our sexual relationship, where Ryan gets frustrated with me, but this is really just symbolic of other broader problems between us. There are many issues that I feel we could work through if we could just talk about it, but Ryan is insistent that we not do so.

In my early life, sex was demanded of and imposed on me, before I was ready and from people with whom sexual contact was not appropriate or helpful. This provided a turbulent and traumatic base to my later sexual and relational life. Later, the constraints of my body hindered my ability to connect sexually, and the damage in my mind also prevented me from finding positive ways of doing so.

I come to realise that without a mutual commitment to communicate and work on our relational issues together, there is nowhere for Ryan and me to go in our relationship, sexually or otherwise. I end the relationship.

Jack and I shared a similar viewpoint on life, but not a similar desire for a relationship. Ryan and I are on completely different wavelengths in many areas, but are both the kind of people to stoically stick to a commitment to make it work; through thick and thin.

At end of the day, I realise that I want both things – loyalty and commitment, as well as a shared worldview and set of values.

I would rather be without a partner at all than be with someone who does not share these priorities combined.

- Eight -

The Turning Point

It's time to heed the call
Time to free-fall from control
And catch yourself in time

Time

You're not prepared to know
You think you got it under control
But life will continue to pass you by, you know

Don't you think it's time
That you started to live?
Don't you think it's time?

You act like love is a one-night stand
An emotion you hold in the palm of your hand
But love will continue to pass you by, you know

Don't you think it's time
That you started to love?
Don't you think it's time?
Don't you think it's time
That you started to live?

It's time to live and grow
It's time, time to know
Time to free-fall from control
And catch yourself in time

The source of life chose to die
Sheer beauty stripped bare in sacrifice
Freedom's voice is calling to you, you know

It's time to live and grow
It's time to heed the call
Time to free-fall from control
And catch yourself in time

Words and Music © Monique Lisbon and Adrian Hannan 2018

When Dr Treloar, the second orthopaedic surgeon I saw, told me that there was no easy way to fix my knee, I asked him if I could have a knee replacement. He replied that it wouldn't work with the amount of weight I carry. Inevitably, I would need another knee replacement within ten or fifteen years, and subsequent knee replacements are never as good as the first. It would only be downhill from there. That was four years ago.

I am forty-eight years old.

What can I do? If I walk even a hundred metres, or stand in the one spot for more than five minutes, the pain is simply unbearable.

I have been taking daily anti-inflammatory tablets ever since then, as well as painkillers several times a day, just to manage to put one foot in front of the other, quite literally.

When I travel by plane, I need to pre-book a wheelchair, as I can't climb the stairs of the plane, and it is too far to walk to the gate lounge.

Now my right knee has started to buckle under my weight also. It's only a matter of time before I will find myself permanently in a wheelchair.

Dr Treloar said that the only solution would be to lose weight. The compassion with which he told me this helped me to hear the truth of what he said. Pointedly, Dr Treloar said that if I did manage to lose weight, I could and probably would regain much of my mobility.

Mobility means independence, choice, freedom.

Two years ago I watched in futile frustration and deep sadness when a friend, about fifteen years older than me, died. Janey had significant respiratory issues and, for the last few years of her life, she felt that not many people – friends or professionals – understood the significance of these issues and the fact that her condition was terminal.

Janey was an extremely talented poet, and we had collaborated together on many creative projects, both hers and mine, over many years. Janey's life meant she understood suffering from the inside, and she brought both the insights of her experience, and her nuanced wordsmithing skills, to bear in helping me shape many CD themes and song lyrics. I also helped her to publish several volumes of poetry – creative offerings that expressed the painful side of life, but which were nonetheless filled with profound beauty.

Janey had survived horrific abuse as a child, and her life's path was far from straightforward. Her poetry was hard-hitting and honest, never glib, but expressing glimpses of hope that constantly surprised and changed her, and brought light and healing to herself and others in the midst of very dark places.

In her final years, I felt powerless to help Janey because she seemed to believe so strongly that there was no way she could get better, or even find any quality of life. She was simply waiting, even planning, to die. For some time, Janey tried to book her own palliative care bed in a hospice, and she felt frustrated when she was repeatedly told that she was not close enough to death to be admitted.

I also felt frustrated because I kept thinking that perhaps Janey could have made different choices for herself, both practical and attitudinal, that may have made her last years not just more bearable but so much more full of quality of life.

In the end, Janey's death seemed sudden and the predominant emotion I felt for quite some months was anger.

Janey, you were too young, and you had survived too many atrocities, to give in and die as you did!

Where did the hope go that had helped you survive those decades of pain, and had been such a gift to others struggling with their own grief and suffering?

Janey, was this really the only option? Why didn't you fight harder? Did you talk yourself into this? And why, with such an amazing gift of crafting words that transformed pain into beauty, did you let go and let the pain take over?

I have felt so guilty about having these thoughts, yet now I wonder whether my anger was actually fuelled by compassion; by a compassionate longing for Janey to have felt embraced by life, even in her 'Gethsemane' days.

And I wonder: was there a point at which Janey could have chosen a different path? Even if, in the end, her health issues were beyond her control, was there a point when she actually decided to give up? Was this the reason her final days were filled with despair and anticipation of death, rather than life?

There have been many times in my life when my friends could have asked the same questions of me. When I took yet another overdose or submitted one more time to the self-hatred that in turn poisoned the way I saw the world and those who sought to love me, could I have chosen differently? When I have felt totally trapped by my circumstances, and powerless to change them, have I been stubbornly refusing to embrace the light, clinging instead to the familiarity of darkness?

As I think about my current situation, I realise that I am now at a crossroads. The crossroads of my choices.

Sandra tells me about a poster displayed outside her local chemist. In the first frame, an old woman is crouched over a walker, her body frail and evidently weighed down with the burden of life. She is all but immobile, literally on her 'last legs'.

In the next frame, the same old woman is crouched over, but this time her body is poised and focussed, ready to dive into a swimming pool.

The caption reads, 'Which life will you choose?'

I am too young to be in a wheelchair, and far too young to die. Which life will I choose?

Nearly being relegated to a wheelchair propels me to choose change. But how on earth can I possibly turn this situation around?

I am forty-eight years old.

I am preparing for the launch of my book, *Keeping Mum*.[7] The timing is perfect for me to have a combined book launch and birthday party.

I want to celebrate both events in style. I contact an old friend, Khloe; a chef extraordinaire, and invite her to cater for the function. Over the phone, I tell Khloe that I want the food to be overflowing and rich, a feast where no-one is left wanting. She suggests we meet in person to plan the finer details.

It's been a couple of years since I last saw Khloe. When I open the door, I can't believe my eyes.

Khloe is the only person I've met who was bigger than me, by about 20kg. We have never talked openly with each other about our issues with weight, while we have shared a silent solidarity in all that we have carried, both physically and emotionally.

Utter transformation greets me. Khloe's warm smile is still the same, and her hug is big and generous as ever. My shock is that it looks like she's lost nearly half of her body!

I have long been aware of an unspoken pact between obese people. We never mention visible signs of lost weight, especially if it's been a long time since we've seen each other. The pact avoids implying that weight is a marker of either vice or virtue. I've also been afraid to compliment other obese people on their weight loss, lest it tap into a psychological insecurity for them. And perhaps they haven't actually lost weight, and my comment will just reinforce a sense of being unacceptable and stuck.

When I see Khloe, I cannot keep my reaction to myself. 'Oh my goodness!' I exclaim. 'You look simply amazing! What happened to you?'

Our discussion about the launch menu is placed on hold, as Khloe and I talk about how she made this transformation happen.

A couple of years ago, Khloe decided to have a 'sleeve gastrectomy'; a form of bariatric or weight loss surgery. This is different from the

---

[7] Monique Lisbon, *Keeping Mum: The Silent Cost of Surviving Childhood Sexual Abuse* (Living Hope Resources: Ashburton, Victoria, 2017)

well-known 'stomach-stapling' or 'lap-banding' procedures. When someone has a gastric sleeve operation, about 80-90% of their stomach is permanently removed, leaving just a tube-like structure; like the 'sleeve' of a shirt.

I have heard all about people who have had lap-bands. Many of them push the constraints of their lap-bands, vomiting regularly, feeling constantly hungry and deprived, and 'cheating' the situation by secretly living on melted ice-cream and Coke. I've heard of people finally having their lap-bands removed after a few years, when they end up heavier than they were before.

My fear of the feeling of deprivation is strong. The book that Khloe is helping me launch is all about my feelings of emotional 'starvation' and neglect by my mother. Perhaps there is no coincidence that the menu Khloe and I are designing for the launch is extravagant; overwhelming in its scope and volume. In my mind, I see a spread like this as an expression of love and positive regard for others. Meagre portions would symbolise a lack of care and attention.

So my fear of deprivation is not merely physical – not even predominantly physical. I fear that if I can't eat a lot, I will also feel emotionally and psychologically deprived.

I know that Khloe will understand these psychological dynamics, so I ask her lots of questions. She tells me she now eats about 10% of what she used to eat, so I ask, 'How can you eat so little without dying of hunger?' I am flabbergasted to hear that she never feels hungry, until she tells me about the effects of having a gastric sleeve on a hormone called 'ghrelin'. In short, ghrelin is a big factor in what makes someone feel hungry:

> Ghrelin is a hormone produced in the gut. It is often termed the hunger hormone, and sometimes called lenomorelin. It travels through your bloodstream and to your brain, where it tells your brain to become hungry and seek out food. Ghrelin's main function is to increase appetite. It makes you consume more food, take in more calories and store fat.[8]

---

8   Rudy Mawer, MSc, CISSN, *Ghrelin: The 'Hunger Hormone' Explained*, 2016, www.healthline.com/nutrition/ghrelin, accessed 25 June 2020.

Khloe tells me that when you have a sleeve gastrectomy, the surgery prevents ghrelin from being secreted and roaming around your body in the same way, so you just don't feel hungry the way you once did.

'But I know I don't eat just because I'm hungry,' I say. 'I eat for a heap of other reasons, most of them emotional.'

'That's what I thought too,' says Khloe, 'and I'm sure that is partly true. But the physical difference is incredible. I used to think about food all the time. Whether I was depriving myself of it, or eating too much of it, it was always uppermost in my mind. Now I just don't experience the same physical prompts to even *think* about food. I actually didn't feel hungry at all for a good year after the surgery. And the lack of hunger shifted my focus away from food. Food started having a more "normal" place in my life – it was one of many enjoyable things, not the main thing I focussed on.'

I still can't believe that such a difference is possible. Yet the proof of the pudding is sitting right in front of my eyes. Khloe has always been beautiful, but her evident confidence and the way she holds herself proudly, complement the physical beauty of her now more well-proportioned body. I see her holding her head high in a way I've never seen in her before. And I feel totally inspired!

Could it really be possible to consume so much less ... without feeling all-consumed by the deprivation and hunger?

I tell Bethany, my general practitioner, about seeing Khloe and what she has shared with me. Bethany refers me to Dr Thoms, a weight loss specialist.

Dr Thoms prescribes the weight-loss medication Saxenda®[9] and I start injecting this drug into my stomach every day for three

---

9 'Saxenda® is an FDA-approved, prescription injectable medicine that, when used with a low-calorie meal plan and increased physical activity, may help some adults with excess weight who also have weight-related medical problems (such as high blood pressure, high cholesterol, or type 2 diabetes), or obesity, to lose weight and keep it off.' (From www.saxenda.com, accessed 25 June 2020.)

months.

In that time, I lose 6kg. Dr Thoms says that I am 'non-responsive' to the medication, losing only 3% of my weight in twelve weeks – 'responsive' patients lose 5-10% of their starting body weight.

I am not at all disheartened by this. Even though I have not lost a great deal of weight on this medication, I have gained something very valuable.

I started on a half-dose of Saxenda® and gradually the dose was increased to full strength. I have been surprised to notice that as the dose increased, my appetite decreased. The difference has been quite tangible. I actually haven't felt like eating as much as I normally would. I have felt full after eating less.

And when I ate less, to my surprise, I found that I didn't feel deprived!

'Maybe this is how a gastric sleeve works?' I say to Bethany. 'Maybe I'll actually feel full eating a lot less! I always thought that if I had bariatric surgery, I'd end up feeling trapped because I'd always be hungry and wanting to eat more without being able to. So I'd end up feeling hungry and deprived, with no way out. What if the surgery actually means I wouldn't *want* to eat more?'

Further consultations with Dr Thoms, and with the surgeon she refers me to, Dr Watson, confirm this thinking. That's exactly how the surgery works, and why it is such an effective tool for weight loss. Evidence shows that it's much more successful, for people who are morbidly obese, than diet and exercise alone.[10]

I am nearly convinced. Like a cloud hanging over me is the enormous place of my psychological issues throughout my life, including my weight gain. If this is simply a physical 'cure', then it won't address the psychological issues that may threaten to undermine and undo the cure. After all, all those people who devour melted ice-cream and Coke, after paying thousands of dollars for a

---

10 See for instance 'Bariatric surgery versus non-surgical treatment for obesity: a systematic review and meta-analysis of randomised controlled trials', BMJ 2013; 347 doi: https://doi.org/10.1136/bmj.f5934 (Published 22 October 2013), accessed 25 June 2020.

surgical fix, surely aren't doing so for physical reasons!

Dr Thoms tells me about a multi-disciplinary outpatient program at the hospital where she works. It includes individual and group sessions with a psychologist, exercise physiologist and dietician.

I register for the program and spend three months intensively preparing emotionally and psychologically for the impact that a sleeve gastrectomy will have on my life. Once again, I am gifted with the informed support of deeply compassionate practitioners, who know all about the challenges and struggles faced by people who have lived with obesity for decades.

By the time 12 January 2018 rolls around, I feel ready for the huge life-change – physically, emotionally and psychologically.

Finally. It's time.

- Nine -

Finding My Feet

Though change takes time
Even change can finally reach its hour

A Thousand Miles

Who knew that a hope unseen
Could more brightly blaze than a fiery sky?
And who knew that a question dared
Could bare far more truth than the answers why?
Seems when screaming beasts are heard and seen
They quickly lose their power
And though change takes time
Even change can finally reach its hour

Who knew, after wandering far
That a homesick heart, at home, could find her place?
And who knew, even fear and shame
Could fall asleep in love's secure embrace?
For when screaming beasts are heard and seen
They quickly lose their power
And though change takes time
Even change can finally reach its hour

Who knew?
To find my feet on solid ground
Brings strength to rise and stand
Who knew?
The journey of a thousand miles
Begins with just one step
Who knew?

Though change takes time
Even change can finally reach its hour

Who knew? …

Well, it seems to me, you always knew
And now I finally know, I know it too

Words © Monique Lisbon 2018
Music © Monique Lisbon and Adrian Hannan 2018
'The journey of a thousand miles …' quotation by Lao Tzu

'**W**hy would you decide to have irreversible surgery in order to lose weight, when there's the choice of just getting a lap-band? Don't you want to have the option to change your mind if it all goes wrong?'

I am forty-eight years old.

I have started telling close friends about my decision to have bariatric surgery, and Dale's question is both common and understandable.

Given how scared I have long been about finding myself trapped in an untenable situation with no way out, maybe I shouldn't opt for having 80 or 90% of my stomach permanently removed? Gastric banding has been around for a long time, and I've heard of many people who have decided, after years of living with a lap-band, that they would prefer to have it removed.

But for me, this question is like asking, 'Why would you get married without a pre-nup in place?'

It has taken me forty-eight years to get to this point. In making the decision to commit myself to losing weight, I now don't want to give myself an 'out'. I know that I do have 'determination and grit', as my mother described it when I was just nineteen – but I also know that I need to do whatever I can to cement my commitment to a positive, informed choice.

For the last three months, I've been attending the multi-disciplinary pre-bariatric surgery program recommended by Dr Thoms; six hours each week. I have learned so much about changing my mindset, starting to exercise, and entirely overhauling my eating habits. And I've also learned about the different types of bariatric surgery, how they work and their relative chances of success.

While managing to lose twenty kilograms since I tipped the scales at around 200kg two years ago, I know that getting to a healthy weight would mean losing more than half my current weight. Apparently even with surgery, I'm highly unlikely to ever lose enough weight to be considered in the 'healthy weight' range. However, with a sleeve gastrectomy, the chance is high of me losing up to 70% of the difference between my heaviest weight and a healthy weight for my height.[11] Since my highest recorded weight was nearly 200kg and my 'ideal' weight is 66kg, I have a high likelihood of losing around 94kg, getting down to just over 100kg.

Nearly half my weight! My mind boggles with the thought!

There is much medical evidence to show that the success rate is higher with a gastric sleeve than with a lap-band, especially for someone with as high a starting weight as mine.

I don't know if the success rate is higher for people after a gastric sleeve than after a lap-band *because* there's no chance of reversal. I do know that, for me, making a permanent, irreversible commitment is important to helping me stick with my resolve to change my life and to follow through with it.

I have seen Khloe's amazing success – and, more to the point, I have heard from her how important it was for her to go into the surgery believing it was possible, and being committed to the changes necessary to make it happen.

I would like to think that if I ever decided to 'throw my lot in' with someone in marriage, I would neither want nor need the option of a pre-nuptial agreement.

In my mind, making an informed and wise choice is about commitment, through thick and thin.

In this case, I'm really hoping that the 'thin' will prevail!

The date is set for surgery. Less than two weeks before Christmas, I begin on a four-week 'very low calorie diet' (VLCD), replacing my normal meals with protein shakes three times a day. Twice a week, I am allowed to supplement my evening 'meal' with ten fresh prawns or 50g of another kind of protein like lean chicken, some steamed vegetables or salad without dressing.

In order for Dr Watson to be able to perform the surgery, my liver needs to be shrunk to provide her with easy access to the part of the stomach she is removing. So this four-week VLCD diet is strict and compulsory.

I finish work for the year on Friday and begin my pre-surgical diet the following day.

Carbohydrates are a deep love; I regularly eat large bowls of pasta or noodles. Pizza is also a mainstay in my diet, and I've been known to eat a whole take-away pizza only hours after finishing a full dinner. Suddenly cutting my intake from well over 3,000 calories per day to less than 500, I feel like my throat has been cut.

By the Sunday night, I am very grumpy and have an intense headache.

When Monday dawns, I feel nauseous with intense hunger and find it hard to get out of bed.

Tuesday arrives and it's time for my final outpatient exercise physiology appointment for the year at my multi-disciplinary program. I feel like fainting, so I stagger out of bed and ring and cancel the session. Then I fall back into bed and start to cry.

This is the first time I have missed one of the sessions in this intensive program, and I feel like a failure. If I can't even pull myself together enough to go and exercise, just four days into this weight loss process, how will I ever be able to last the distance, which will take years?

Have I made a terrible mistake? Can I really do this? Is it too late to back out now?

Dr Watson made it very clear that if my liver did not shrink enough in the four weeks before the surgery, she may be unable to operate as planned. This is not a punitive threat, just a medical fact. So I roll over in bed, and try to block out my hunger, fear and sense of failure.

Eating my ten fresh prawns that night, I savour each one as never before, rolling each morsel repeatedly over my tongue. They taste *so damn good!*

By the end of a long and testing week, I experience a great sense of relief as I realise I have finally reached 'ketosis'.[12]

---

12 'Ketosis is a natural metabolic state. It involves the body producing ketone bodies

Khloe told me that this blissful day would come – one of the only things that has helped me hang in there during the last week of hell, when my body has, quite literally, been in starvation mode.

My body has realised that there are no carbohydrates left to burn, and it has finally started to burn fat instead.

The numbers have been rapidly dropping on the bathroom scales all week, but now an equally tangible outcome comes – a sense of relief from no longer feeling ravenous twenty-four hours a day.

Christmas falls on the following Monday, and I am invited to spend it with my friend Leah and her family. Leah is aware that I need to stick to a very strict dietary regime before my surgery and she has applied her creative and culinary skills to carve a Christmas tree from a large cucumber, complete with carrot star, beautifully placed atop a platter of snow peas, cherry tomatoes, capsicum, spinach leaves, radishes and a smattering of shavings of Christmas ham. I feel deeply supported, and thoroughly enjoy the abundant love that underpins the preparation of the sparse spread.

The dietician I see as part of the bariatric surgery program tells me that in getting through these four weeks, I have survived the hardest part of the process, physically speaking.

I know that enduring the physical struggle was only possible because of the strength I've gained from surviving the decades of emotional turmoil that led up to this point.

When the day of the surgery arrives, I feel ready to fully embrace a new way of life.

And what a new way of life it is!

The first and most noticeable change is physical. Coming out of the surgery, I am surprised at my reaction to my first meal the next day – a protein milk drink. Rather than thinking the meal too

---

out of fat, and using them for energy instead of carbs. You can get into ketosis by following a very low-carb, high-fat ketogenic diet … To go into ketosis, people generally need to eat fewer than 50 grams of carbs per day and sometimes as little as 20 grams per day.' (www.healthline.com/nutrition/what-is-ketosis, accessed 4 July 2020)

small, I feel astonished that I am expected to be able to drink such a large glass of fluid. Over the course of an hour, a sip at a time, I manage to drink half of the glass, and then feel totally full and unable to drink any more.

After bariatric surgery, it's important to build up very slowly in terms of food intake. For the first two weeks after the operation, all of my food is vitamised, as I can't stomach any solids. Then for the remainder of that month, I manage to eat puréed foods, like baby food – but only tiny quantities. I feel totally full eating a tenth of what I used to eat, and sometimes have to force myself to finish eating my meagre meals.

By the time I get to eat about a quarter of a scrambled egg, I can't believe how glorious it tastes! A throw-back to my VLCD prawns before surgery, I savour every tiny morsel of egg. Has food ever tasted this good? I do not feel at all deprived – rather, I feel richly and amply sated with very, very little.

Coming home from hospital and rehab, and moving slowly from puréed foods to soft solids, I am keen to expand my dietary repertoire, and repeatedly push myself beyond the limits. It takes a while to learn to remember to eat very slowly, and to wait for my brain to realise that my stomach is full. During these weeks, eating even half a teaspoon too much means the difference between being able to comfortably swallow and enjoy the food, and feeling intensely uncomfortable, or even throwing up.

It is a steep learning curve, but a necessary one, to listen to my body and heed its signals. Having come from a time and place where I could easily devour a whole pizza an hour after a large dinner, adapting to the far finer distinctions of just a few grams of food is a new and subtle art. The negative reinforcement of the discomfort when I push my eating beyond my limits is a good motivator to learn to heed the signs. Yet this alone would not suffice to enable me to permanently change my habits, unless I also experienced positive reinforcement.

For the first six months, I lose, on average, between six and eight kilograms per month. I feel an incredible sense of achievement whenever I step on the scales, as the numbers keep dropping in such large increments.

Friends soon start noticing the difference, and their affirmation and encouragement also provide positive reinforcement.

Most of all, I feel on a 'roll'. As the weight loss continues in a consistent and relatively dramatic way, I feel spurred on to continue. The thing that feels most incredible is the fact that I am now eating only a small fraction of what I used to eat, but I never, *never*, feel hungry. 'Deprivation' is not a word that would even occur to me as a descriptor of my experience. As time goes on, and the stomach inflammation settles from the surgery, the variety of foods I can now eat, expands. I can even manage small amounts of pasta or rice. Having just five strands of spaghetti feels so much more bountiful and extravagantly rich than the old regime of huge bowls of pasta. I do not feel at all deprived … rather, I feel spoilt, nourished and nurtured. It simply takes a lot less food, and vastly different types of foods, to achieve this feeling.

Occasionally I see people who I haven't seen for six or twelve months, and they are shocked to see the difference in me – just as I was astounded the day Khloe first knocked on my door after her dramatic weight loss. The question is always the same: 'How on earth did you do it?'

The first few times I'm asked this question, I reply by saying that I've had a gastric sleeve. Then I realise that, alone, this is not the answer at all. The gastric sleeve is not what has made me 'do it' – rather, it is what has made my weight loss effort 'doable'. The surgery is neither the beginning nor the end of the journey; rather, a crucial gateway from one way of being into a different future.

It took me decades to start to understand and grapple with the issues that led me to gain so much weight in the first place, and to compound my struggles to lose it for so many years. Those issues were largely emotional and psychological, and were later reinforced by physical limitations and behaviours. Reaching the gateway of my bariatric surgery was the result of a long preceding path, full of seemingly contradictory twists and turns.

The journey on the other side is similarly complex, and needs to be navigated from several different angles – emotional, psychological, relational and physical.

Exercise is an indelibly important component in weight loss. Having carried so much weight, I had never been able to exercise much without enormous discomfort and even pain. But now, as the kilograms drop, the burden on my vulnerable knees and back also decreases. I am introduced to hydrotherapy as a means of non-weight bearing exercise, and fall in love with being in the water.

In the past whenever I've pushed myself, or felt pushed by others, to exercise to the point of puffing or sweating, the experience has felt not just uncomfortable, but deeply distressing. The larger I got, the more quickly I would feel winded by even the slightest degree of exertion, and this breathlessness felt akin to the panic attacks that pervaded my twenties, when I was regularly moving in and out of psychiatric hospitals. The physical experiences of being puffed out also triggered memories of abuse, which made me feel trapped and totally out of control of my body.

Fear of these triggers led me to become more and more sedentary. The negative associations with physical exertion were strong and deeply rooted, and I would do anything to avoid them.

Now that I have less of a load to carry, I do not feel the same degree of breathlessness when I move. To my surprise and delight, I am buoyed by the water, and comforted by the warmth of the hydrotherapy pool. Having spent the last decade or more barely able to walk on land, I find that I can not only walk, but can even jog in the water!

After my hydrotherapy sessions, initially ten or fifteen minutes long, then twenty, thirty, forty minutes, and eventually an hour at a time, I feel a satisfied and comfortable exhaustion. Having struggled incessantly with insomnia, I now find myself sleeping more deeply and restfully during the nights after I've exercised. I feel doubly good – there is my pride in the virtue of completing an exercise workout, alongside the physical affirmation of a body that feels increasingly healthy and enjoys moving. People have always told me that exercise is addictive, and that it releases endorphins that help lift your mood. I just never believed them.

To my great surprise, the small initial changes quickly pick up pace and I find the results start to increase exponentially.

I dare to lean into the trust that I can increase my fitness, and embrace a new way of being physically present in the world, and am rewarded for this trust by greater weight loss.

More important than the decreasing numbers on the scales, I start to find that I enjoy being a physical being. My body stops feeling like a repository of shame, fear, powerlessness and passivity, and starts to feel active, strong and alive.

After some months, I find that the smallest clothes in the 'big girl' shops are now too large for me, and I start shopping in 'normal' clothes stores. Initially I seek out smaller versions of the old kinds of clothes I used to wear – clothes that would hide my body. It takes a long time before I realise that along with being able to choose smaller clothes, I can now choose clothes that actually show off my body, and even hug it tightly.

My wardrobe shifts from being filled with disguises for my sense of shame, to being filled with lovely celebrations of my pride.

It is just after New Year's Day. I have now lost 67kg since the surgery, and a total of 91kg since my highest recorded weight several years earlier.

I am nearly fifty years old.

When I weigh in with Bethany, I'm delighted to see that even with the festive season celebrations, I have still lost a further 3kg.

In the height of summer holidays I have been going to the pool more often; every day or two.

'I think my pool jogging has really helped,' I say to Bethany.

'You know,' she says, 'It can be a good thing to mix up your exercise a bit. As well as the potential of getting bored with doing the same kind of exercise, your body can also end up getting somewhat complacent, and stop responding to exercise in the same way. Have you ever thought of walking?'

'Walking?!' I quip, 'Out in nature? What a horrible idea!'

I speak in jest, but I am aware there is a strong element of seriousness behind my words. I actually feel scared to walk out in the 'real world'. Walking or jogging in the confines of the swimming pool feels safe. Walking outside means feeling a lot less contained. I remember many times when I've found myself needing to walk alongside friends on the street. I have always felt embarrassed and humiliated by the ways I puff and pant after even very short distances, finding it so difficult to keep up with others. I also think back to the daily walks with my parents in my teenage years. Even though my father ensured we avoided walking in the 'dirty' nature reserve, walking along the streets, with overhanging trees on the sides of the road, also felt uncomfortable to me.

When I leave Bethany's office, I realise that I need to challenge my assumption that walking in nature would feel uncomfortable. I ring Leah and suggest we go for a walk together, down to the beach near her house. She is also on holidays and readily agrees.

As we walk together, I am surprised to find that not only can I keep up with Leah, at times I need to slow my gait so that she can keep up with me. Leah has also struggled with her weight over the years but, at her peak, she has always been about half of my size. We are now a similar weight, and we talk readily and easily about our weight and bodies, and about the changes that I've undergone over the last year. It feels so different to be out walking with Leah. The sun is warm and I feel bathed in nourishment and nurture in the same way as the water from the pool buoys me up and carries me through my steps. No longer feeling acutely embarrassed and uncomfortable from minimal physical exertion, I now feel free to take in my surroundings.

Nature is not horrible after all. It is glorious. There is so much beauty to take in, now that I can see and imbibe the world beyond the walls of my prison-body.

This marks the beginning of a new daily routine – walking outside. I now see the beauty of the trees, hear the birds, and experience the warmth and nurture of the sun's rays on my bare arms. As I walk, rather than feeling puffed, I experience an extraordinary feeling, like I'm floating on air. I liken this feeling to walking on a 'travellator' at the airport. How far and how quickly I can glide through space, with so little effort. Without the load of an extra ninety-odd kilograms on my shoulders, I feel light and free.

My sense of freedom is expanded by an amazing sense of achievement. I have now lost as much weight as my surgeon said I would ever be likely to lose – 70% of my excess weight. Anything from here is a bonus, and beyond anyone's expectations. I am also approaching the point of having halved my body. I feel proud, but also daunted, by the prospect of being less than half my size.

The words from my mother's letter at the age of nineteen return to my mind: 'I can guarantee you that you will feel better half your size.' At the time of the letter, I weighed around 70kg, so losing half my weight would likely have ended my life. I carried those words inside me for many years, as a tacit statement that my mother wished I was dead. I embraced this desire to disappear, to no longer be present to disturb and disappoint my mother. I have come to see that I put on weight in the years since to try to thwart her expectations and hopes that I might conveniently 'waste away'.

Ironically, however, she is right – having got to the weight I eventually did, I do now feel better half my size. I feel better, and more OK in the world and in my own skin, than I could ever have believed was possible.

It has been said, 'The journey of a thousand miles begins with just one step.'[13] It took me nearly fifty years to feel equipped to take that first step. Now I feel propelled from strength to strength, step to step, mile to mile.

I purchase a Fitbit and start tracking my daily steps. By the end of May, I am delighted to realise that in the course of the last five months, I have literally walked a thousand miles.

---

13 Quotation by Lao Tzu.

- Ten -

Learning to Fly

I wanna live
Deliberately

Deliberately

I wanna live, wanna live deliberately
Don't wanna find, I've just lived superficially
I wanna live, wanna live deliberately

Embracing my shadow
Questioning the light
I wanna live, wanna live deliberately

Seeking out the marrow
Till I'm teeming with life
I wanna live, wanna live deliberately

To dance life
Revere life
To hold life bare
Caress life
Confess life
To live, to dare!

I wanna live, wanna live deliberately …

Words and Music © Monique Lisbon 2005
after Henry David Thoreau (1817-1862)

At the end of last year, part of the multi-disciplinary pre-bariatric surgery support program I attended involved hydrotherapy. There was an indoor pool at the rehabilitation hospital where the program was held, and I loved being supported in my exercises there, both by the buoyant water and by the exercise physiologists who encouraged me.

I am forty-nine years old.

After my bariatric surgery, I returned to this hospital, being admitted for support in the inpatient rehabilitation unit rather than returning home to an empty house. Once my wounds had healed enough, I revelled in the water once again.

The hydrotherapy pool is indoors, tucked away behind the sheltered gym where patients learn to get back on their feet after an injury or an illness like a stroke. Safety and support are the key dynamics of this place, and for me it was so important to find my feet in a safe, supported environment.

I knew I needed to find a way to feel safe and supported, moving and exercising, out in the 'wider world'.

When my time ended in the rehabilitation program, I joined a pool about ten minutes' drive from my house. There is actually another pool closer to home. Intentionally, I don't go there. I do not feel ready to see neighbours, acquaintances or friends from my old church or workplace. I would rather start my new life of exercise where I'm less likely to run into anyone I know.

It's Friday evening and I'm back at the pool. I've been coming to the indoor hydrotherapy pool here for a couple of months now. I really enjoy it, but there are many more people coming and going, which means there isn't the same sense of security as I experienced at the rehab hospital, where I regularly saw the same small group of patients.

I have taken a printout of the program created for me at the rehab hospital, and purchased equipment to ensure I can keep following the prescribed exercises.

On a roll, I am in the routine of coming here several times a week. Attending late in the evening means it's dark outside, so the fluorescent lights in the pool highlight my reflection in the floor-to-ceiling windows that separate the hydrotherapy pool from the carpark outside.

For years I've avoided cameras and mirrors, always hating what I saw. Now I catch a glimpse of my reflected self in the darkened glass wall, walking back and forth along the length of the pool, water weights in hand. I feel proud of myself for being able to do this! What's more, I find it hard to believe, but looking at my reflection, I don't even think I stick out anymore! My body is still larger than some of the other people at the pool, but not conspicuously so.

I dare to think to myself, 'Perhaps I can just blend in now – I might have already lost enough kilos that in the water, people can't even notice that I'm overweight?'

This is a totally new thought to me. I have always known that I stick out. Blending in has never been in the realms of possibility for me, so instead I've just tried to avoid places where it feels humiliating or embarrassing to be different.

I smile as I think about the possibility of looking 'normal'; simply one of the crowd.

Just then, a man comes up to me in the water. I have seen him at the pool a couple of times before, but we've never talked.

Still smiling, I say to him, 'Hi! Isn't it glorious being in the water tonight?'

Rather than respond to my superficial comment, or even introduce himself to me, the man launches straight in: 'Hi. I can see that you struggle with your weight. A friend of mine is overweight too, and she has recently found out that she has problems with her thyroid …'

An internal alarm has just sounded at a thousand decibels. I can't quite take in that this man thinks that it's appropriate to say something like this to a total stranger. If I had my wits about me, I would tell him so, but I don't. The smile drops from my face and I try to move away from him in the water without saying anything. He follows me. Through a haze, I can hear his continuing chatter about his friend's health issues, and I feel angry and violated.

How could I have thought I might ever appear normal while out in public, especially being half-naked with strangers in a swimming pool?

Will I ever feel safe enough to come back again?

The year chugs along, and I continue to visit the pool, several times a week. My friend Dale makes a great pool buddy. When we arrange times for me to pick her up to take her to the pool for a workout, I know that, because she doesn't drive, if I cancel our visits she will also miss out. So my commitment to transporting her to the pool helps me keep on track also. It's a win-win for both of us.

I enjoy Dale's company enormously. Having been one of the few friends I shared with about planning to have a sleeve gastrectomy before it actually happened, she's also been a great encouragement to me as I've continued to lose weight in the months since.

On the phone Dale says, 'I've got a surprise for you, which I'll give you when I see you next. I'm really excited about it, and think you'll love it!'

I am curious and excited to see what she is going to give me. A few days later, as we are driving to the pool, Dale shares her surprise.

'I went to a clothes store that has fashions for larger women. I was talking to the shop assistant and she told me about a free service they offer, to help larger people define their own personal clothing style. I told her about your amazing weight loss and she gave me this brochure to give you, suggesting you come in for a free consultation!'

Dale's voice is animated and excited.

I am glad that it is dark in the car. Hopefully the darkness means Dale can't see the tears that are welling up in my eyes. I try to hide them as I force out the words, 'Oh great, thanks Dale. That's really thoughtful. I'll have a look at the brochure later.'

Dale had never been to this clothes shop before, and when she happened across it, she thought this was a wonderful service for larger people. And it really does sound like a great service.

What Dale clearly doesn't realise is that I haven't had the option of shopping for clothes anywhere other than this store – or other stores like it – for decades! And now, finally, I am starting to be able to buy 'normal' clothes, so this is the last place I would want to go back to.

I remember seeing the Tom Hanks film *Castaway*, several years ago. The main character, Chuck, gets stranded on a desert island and needs to find a way to survive for years on his own. His only semblance of company is a volleyball, which he personifies and names 'Wilson', fashioning it into a living being in his mind, to avoid going crazy with the years of isolation. Chuck is finally rescued from the desert island, after years of surviving on an extremely limited diet of whatever he can forage or catch from the ocean.

When he returns, Chuck's sense of alienation from the rest of the world, including his fiancée, is profound. No-one really knows or understands what Chuck has been through, and what it has taken for him to survive. This sense of alienation, difference, and lack of understanding, is poignantly symbolised by the fact that at his homecoming party, the buffet contains only seafood. Succulent prawns and lobster would be a rich treat in any other context, while they are the last thing Chuck wants or needs to welcome him back to the 'real world'.

When Dale gives me the brochure for the larger women's clothes shop styling consultation service, I feel like I am being offered prawns and lobster after years of eating nothing but seafood. The offering is lovely and, in any other context, would be wonderfully welcome. Yet for me, having just started to enter the 'normal' world and finally being able to fit into clothes off the rack, this is the last thing I want.

I don't doubt that Dale's gift comes from a genuine and encouraging place, and that she wants nothing but the best for me. I know that she has suggested this as an encouragement to me to keep moving forward. But it highlights for me just how hard it is for others, who have not lived inside a body like mine, to understand the place I've come from and the subtleties of moving to a different place of being.

It is eight months since my gastric sleeve operation and I have now lost 70kg,

I am forty-nine years old.

For the last few months, I've been having dizzy spells, accompanied by sudden drops in blood pressure and sudden increases in my heart rate. These episodes can occur up to five times a day. Generally they pass within a minute or two and, though they are intensely uncomfortable, I can ride them through without anyone noticing. Occasionally however, I have dropped things I've been holding or fallen over in a semi-faint.

Bethany has referred me to a cardiologist, as she is concerned that I might have 'postural orthostatic tachycardia syndrome' (POTS).[14] Having been on medication for high blood pressure for years, I find it highly ironic that I am now being investigated for low blood pressure.

The cardiologist takes a history and runs some tests. He confirms that I do, in fact, have a form of 'POTS'. However, he is reassuring that mine is not the true 'neurologically-based' version of the syndrome, for which there are some treatments, but no cure.

---

14 'Postural orthostatic tachycardia syndrome (POTS) is a condition in which a change from lying to standing causes an abnormally large increase in heart rate. This occurs with symptoms that may include lightheadedness, trouble thinking, blurred vision or weakness … The causes of POTS are varied. Often, it begins after a viral infection, surgery or pregnancy. Risk factors include a family history of the condition. Diagnosis in adults is based on an increase in heart rate of more than 30 beats per minute within ten minutes of standing up which is accompanied by symptoms. Treatment may include avoiding factors that bring on symptoms, increasing dietary salt and water, compression stockings, exercise, cognitive behavioral therapy (CBT) and medications.' (See https://en.wikipedia.org/wiki/Postural_orthostatic_tachycardia_syndrome, accessed 8 July 2020).

Rather, he tells me that I have an 'acquired' form of POTS, as my body is simply struggling to adapt to the rapid weight loss. The good news is that once my weight stabilises, the episodes should decrease in frequency and intensity.

He sends me for an echocardiogram to confirm that there is no underlying damage to my heart, and that the years of strain from my obesity have not caused permanent heart damage.

I am relieved when these tests come back clear. Although the episodes continue to be uncomfortable, and I need to be careful to avoid falling over when they occur, it does help me to know that the blood pressure drops and escalated heart rate are just my body's way of responding to rapid and intense physical change.

This is one more thing I need to try to adapt to while I am losing weight. For many years, I have worked so hard psychologically to cut off from my body. My body carried many effects of my trauma and psychological distress, but I managed to push my body largely out of my consciousness. Even when I felt completely trapped in the constraints and pain of my body, I simultaneously pushed an awareness of my body far from my mind.

So, finally coming into my body, learning to live inside it, is a very new phenomenon. For much of the time, it is exciting to be exploring new and positive ways of having a body – enjoying movement and exercise, buying smaller and more flattering clothes, getting in touch with healthy ways of eating and feeling richly satisfied with much less food. Yet there are also uncomfortable dynamics, such as these dizzy spells, that are a very real part of becoming 'embodied'.

In past years, when I felt anxious or stressed, I would be overwhelmingly aware of the emotional overload long before I realised that my body was affected.

Now, I find that these dizzy spells alert me to the fact that I'm stressed, often before I have even realised or felt it emotionally.

A new dialogue has begun between my mind, emotions and body. Pathways that were once completely cut off are now opening, and the communication can be at times disconcerting and uncomfortable.

Just like my thoughts and emotions, my body has something to tell me. My body is not an inferior part of me, to be subdued and suppressed. Rather, it is a source of wisdom – and I realise I need to listen to it, deliberately, if I am to learn to heed what it tells me.

Growing used to the new channels of communication between my mind, emotions and body, I am learning not just what feels bad in my body, but also what feels good.

I am fifty years old.

Two years ago I made a big financial investment and had a hot tub installed in my backyard. Wanting to make the most of it, I spent a lot of time, money and energy setting it up to be a gorgeous and luxurious oasis. Decking was built around the tub and remote-controlled café blinds created an instantly secure and private space. Leah and I attended a one-day lead-lighting workshop to make two panels which were then installed in the clear pergola overhead, offset with a string of small lights to illuminate the stained glass at night-time. I spent a couple of months designing and making a two-panel coloured glass mosaic installation, around 1.5m tall, which overlooks the hot tub on the beautifully painted wall, featuring five shades of blue and several colourful sea creatures. A motley collection of hanging ornaments – glass, sparkling, metallic, colourful – creates a mystical canopy under the pergola, each dancing in the breeze, some with peaceful tinkling sounds. A large screen TV and musical sound system treat the senses, and a wall of fairy lights completes the magical space.

After the hot tub was installed I jokingly said to my friend Richard, 'Well, this is my investment in hedonism and decadence', to which he cheekily replied, 'You mean, your investment in health and wellbeing, don't you?'

Over time, Richard's interpretation has proved correct. Unlike many people who have pools or hot tubs installed and never use them, it is very rare for a day to go by when I do not have at least one soak in the tub, often having a dip two or even three times a day.

The tub has also become a source of socialising, and I love inviting friends to sit in the warm water and experience the ambience and relaxation with me.

Just as increasing my exercise has settled my insomnia and created longer and more restful slumber, I also find that having a soak in the hot tub last thing at night before I retire is a great way to unwind and ensure I'm ready for a good night's sleep.

All of this is very new for me. For many years, through the worst of my recovery from abuse, I either pushed my body beyond its limits, ignored its needs and neglected it, or punished it with many and varied self-harming actions. To invest in – and enjoy – nurturing, nourishing and treating my body to good things, is a huge shift for me.

Having worked hard to create and embrace a new and healthier body, I am now learning how to 'fly' in that body; honouring it by investing in my own health and wellbeing.

- Eleven -

A Tender Dance

I couldn't do it without me
I couldn't do it without you

Me and You

Had it all been up to me
Would have never come this far
A marathon of many miles
Can only cover so much ground
To reach the highest peak
Is half the victory alone
And the beauty of the view
Is doubled when it's shared

Had it all been up to you
Would have never come this far
If I'd been carried all the way
My feet would never find the ground
The strength that drives me on
Has grown within my bones
And the air I deeply breathe
Is the life within my heart

When I fall down, you pick me up
When I fly, you soar with me
You gently hold my heart
As I endure, as I let go
I couldn't do it without me
I couldn't do it without you
A tender dance of toil and grace
Together, me and you

I strive to keep on moving
A living journey shared
I seek to rest my soul
In the steady hands of love

When I fall down …

Words © Monique Lisbon 2019
Music © Monique Lisbon and Adrian Hannan 2019

Growing used to my 'new' body is a continuing struggle.
I am fifty years old.

At the same time as experiencing an unprecedented sense of freedom, mobility and independence, I keep thinking that one day I'll wake up and the positive changes will have all been a dream. I will be back, trapped, in a world and a body over which I have little control.

When I enter clothes stores, instinctively I gravitate towards the largest clothes on the racks. I frequently try on clothes two or three sizes too large, before remembering that my body is different now, and requires smaller sizes.

These changes, while delightful, are also unsettling. I've been fast making a home inside a transformed body, yet it still doesn't feel my own. In short, I can't trust who I am and the frame that holds me.

I have always tended towards processing my feelings externally. It has taken me many years to get to a point of being able to sit alone with uncomfortable feelings and process them internally. My first instinct is always to talk through important or difficult things with trusted others.

This exciting and vulnerable time in my life is no different. Friends contact me with encouraging emails, text messages, phone calls and cards, and I also reach out to them regularly with text and email updates. It's as if I need to constantly 'check' my new reality. The changes feel surreal and checking in with others I trust is a way for me to have confidence in the person I am becoming.

Within one week, I reach three symbolic milestones. First, I have now lost 100kg in total. Second, I have dropped below the 100kg mark; down into double-figures. Third, I am about to reach the point of weighing half of my highest ever recorded weight.

I text a few friends to share my news. Two of them respond

quickly with their reliable and consistent encouragement. The third friend, Leah, does not.

I wait for several days before sending Leah a second text message, asking if she received my first message. She tells me she did, without responding to the content.

We finally talk about it on the phone. Leah and I both value authenticity and openness, so I try to listen without defensiveness as she talks bluntly with me.

She asks, frustrated: 'Why do you need affirmation from others? It's like a teenager asking her girlfriends, "Do I look fat in this dress?"'

Leah says she felt manipulated by my message, and hadn't responded because she didn't feel free to make a genuine response. Rather, she felt pressured to say what I wanted her to say.

Leah also explains that she has been feeling increasingly negative about herself after bingeing on leftover birthday food, and my text message felt like salt in the wound.

Then she says, 'You ask me what I thought when I got your message? Well, to be honest, I thought, "Great. *Even Mono* is now smaller than me!"'

These words sting. Did Leah think that I could never achieve what I have now, in fact, achieved? Even as she encouraged me in my weight loss, was she only feigning support, never believing that 'even Mono' could actually get this far? Am I so different from her and everyone else that it would be impossible for me to ever reach a point of just fitting in?

Despite my hurt, I sit with Leah's words for a couple of days, trying to not just dismiss what she has told me; instead to be open to taking on board anything I need to look at and change in myself.

Debriefing with my friend Khloe, she says: 'I know what it feels like to have friends respond to your weight loss in that way. I was really surprised by the reactions I got from different people. Some friends were so encouraging and supportive – but some, both those who were overweight and those who weren't – seemed to really hate seeing me lose weight. It was almost like they felt that if I succeeded, that would mean they had failed.

'It's a real pity that Leah couldn't have just said to you, "Please don't send me messages like this for the time being. I'm having trouble being pleased for you, because it just highlights how bad I'm feeling about myself."

'At least if she had said something like that, then you would know it's her issue, not yours. And there's absolutely nothing manipulative about you having shared your news – it's up to her to tell you if she doesn't want to, or can't, hear it.'

Khloe's words help me let go of a sense of self-blame. They also highlight something I have not previously realised. Leah's comments might not be about me at all – they might simply be an expression of her own issues. When I push her to express a reaction to my experiences, I need to be willing to hear whatever she genuinely feels, if we are to have an honest relationship.

Yet I still find it hard not to take Leah's response personally; as a statement of me being unacceptably different. For so many years, as I've struggled with being massively overweight and the object of perceived or actual judgment from others, I have felt like an alien. There have been very few others in my life who could understand my particular sense of vulnerability from the inside.

My sense of being 'different' from everyone else continuously escalated and led me to lose touch with the fact that no-one escapes having insecurities and vulnerabilities. I hadn't grasped the fact that Leah might feel a sense of failure or negativity about her body, even though in retrospect I realise she has alluded to this many times before. Leah has always been so much smaller than me, and she's also always talked in a very matter-of-fact way about her shape and size, never trying to hide it, even making a point of joking about it and flaunting it at times. So I saw myself as different from Leah just as I felt different from everyone else around me.

I am now facing a new way of being 'different'. It has been reported that two-thirds of Australians are over a healthy weight. For the first time in my life, I am now in a healthy minority. It is hard for me to fathom that having lost nearly two-thirds of my body, I have now also lost my shared place with two-thirds of the population.

Inch by Inch

So even while I felt alien and different from others when I was obese, I was in good company. I've come to realise that many people's internal body issues are externally invisible and cannot be measured from the outside. Even those with a relatively 'normal' body are not necessarily immune from psychological insecurity and vulnerability.

Reaching out to Leah with regular updates, ceases. She has not directly asked me to stop, but I realise that it is not helpful for either her or me, if I give this degree of detail about my inner world, unless she asks me to share. Instead I try to listen more to what is going on for her, and to be present to her, understanding that not everyone's feelings and issues are always about me.

I also want to acknowledge that, whatever our size and shape, to a lesser or greater degree, our bodies can be a source of vulnerability for all of us.

Talking with Cheryl about my weight loss progress emphasises diverse perspectives.

Cheryl and I have been friends for more than half our lives, having both been part of the same Christian group at university in our early twenties. We have caught up over a meal every few months for decades.

Cheryl knew and loved me at 70kg, she knew and loved me at 140kg, and she knew and loved me at 200kg.

I am fifty-one years old.

It's been a few months since we last saw each other, and I'm visiting her for a belated birthday lunch.

Cheryl is standing on her porch as I pull into her driveway. When she sees me, she starts laughing gleefully and clapping her hands. Then she comes over to the car and envelops me in a huge bear-hug.

'What are you laughing at?' I ask.

'You're smaller than me!!' she replies, laughing with pure delight.

Over lunch, Cheryl tells me several things she hasn't told me before. Whenever I used to visit her, she would book a local café for us to meet at. She tells me now that she was always aware of how difficult I found it to walk in from the carpark and up any stairs. She noticed that it was hard for me to find my way to the table if I had to weave between other tables and people. So she tells me that she intentionally chose cafés with easy access. She would always arrive early and choose a table close to the door, so that I didn't have to travel far or move awkwardly to sit down. And she would only choose cafés with booth seats and moveable tables, or with chairs without arms, so that I would always be able to sit comfortably and without embarrassment.

It is a total surprise to me to hear this. Cheryl had never let me know any of these considerate measures she had taken to try to ensure I never felt out of place or at the receiving end of judgment when my body was so much bigger. She worked hard to ensure I felt as comfortable physically as I did in the warm embrace of her friendship.

Cheryl also tells me that for a long period, whenever I left after one of our lunches, she would worry, and she would grieve. She realised each time that this might be the last time she would see me. She recognised that the strain my weight was placing on my heart and other parts of my body, might result in a premature death.

Cheryl never told me about these fears while I was overweight. She was always attentive to my descriptions of the inner and outer movements in my life, and encouraging and supportive of any positive changes I made, but she felt that it would not help for her to put pressure on me to change. She knew that I knew that I needed to change – and she trusted and believed I would do so when I was ready and able.

These words from Cheryl do not surprise me. Since I have lost weight, others have also told me that they had been afraid that medical complications from my obesity might kill me in the end. I feel deeply saddened by what Cheryl has told me, but also find it a great source of comfort. It highlights the fact that my friends love me deeply, and their compassion, concern – and now celebration – all spring from that love and care.

Inch by Inch

I am fifty years old.

My eldest niece, Anna, is getting married tomorrow.

It's been six years since I saw last her, after cutting ties with my brother and sister-in-law. For many complex reasons, I felt I had no choice but to sever my relationship with Grant and Margaret. However, losing my relationships with their daughters, my three nieces, has been a source of deep and profound grief for me.

I have tried and tried to think of a way in which I could re-establish relationships with my nieces, whilst maintaining the safe distance I believed I needed from Grant and Margaret. It has never felt possible.

My love for my nieces has never wavered, and it has been particularly hard to lose them from my life.

I have sent Anna and her fiancé a wedding present and a card, trying to express my deep love for and pride in Anna, and my longing to be able to be there physically to celebrate this milestone. I know that there are no words that can easily convey the reasons I feel I can't be there, and I shed tears as I write and send the card and gift.

Attending the wedding would mean seeing all the members of my family who I made excruciating decisions to cut off from – seeing my father for the first time in twenty years, my mother for the first time in four years, and Grant and Margaret for the first time in six years.

If only there were a way I could be there! ...

But, on the night before the big day, I know I just can't.

I wake early on Anna's wedding day. Both Anna and my brother send me text messages, letting me know that, if I change my mind and decide to come, there will be a place for me at the wedding and reception.

Sandra is on leave at the moment, so I have a session scheduled with another therapist who I occasionally see whenever Sandra is away.

I discuss the situation with this therapist, and decide that, with certain boundaries in place, I do feel strong enough to go. I am aware that the emotional fallout might be huge, and that I may find myself back at the bottom of a deep psychological hole. Yet my love for Anna and my longing to be there, make me decide to take that risk.

When I leave the therapy session, I find my mother has left me a voicemail message. Her words are stilted and uncomfortable. It is clearly a big effort for her to make the call, and I know that she too is taking a risk in doing so. She apologises for breaching my privacy but asks me to consider coming to the wedding, rather than miss out on such an important family event.

I ring Ryan to let him know what I've decided to do. He is currently working a couple of hours out of town, and he is also due to fly out tonight for a week to visit another interstate client. Ryan and I have only been seeing each other for a month, so I am astonished when he offers to drive back to accompany me to the wedding – and to delay his interstate trip tonight if I decide I want to stay for the reception.

I send my mother, my brother and Anna text messages, letting them know I will be there for the wedding, but not the reception. It is already a huge thing for me to contemplate going to the wedding. It is helpful for me to be able to say that my partner needs to fly out tonight, as this gives me an escape strategy if I find I'm not coping.

One of the other strategies that the therapist has suggested is to remain as distant and matter-of-fact as I can when greeting my family. She suggested that I relate to them politely, like acquaintances. And if they project into the situation the assumption that I am there to seek reconciliation with them, I should firmly and politely say, 'I just didn't want to miss this important day for Anna.'

When I arrive at the wedding, any such plans fly out the window.

As soon as Margaret sees me, her eyes fill with tears and she grips me in a bear-hug as though her life depended on it. 'I have prayed so hard for this moment, Mono. This is such an answer to prayer,' she says.

'I just didn't want to miss this important day for Anna,' I reply, and it is true, but the words are not spoken as a polite acquaintance. Tears are flowing freely for me also. I try several times to move from her embrace, but Margaret will not let me go.

Then I see my mother. She too is crying, and she buries her head in her hands and rocks back and forward, wailing like a Greek grandmother. I have only ever seen my mother cry a handful of times in my life, which makes her emotion at this time all the more raw and powerful.

'I can't believe it,' she says. 'I just can't believe it.'

My stunningly gorgeous, mature, adult niece Anna is accompanied on her sojourn up the altar by four bridesmaids. I recognise my middle niece Diana, also sophisticated and now all grown-up, and I survey the other three bridesmaids. Through a process of elimination, I work out which one is my youngest niece Gabriella. Gab was only ten the last time I saw her; now sixteen. So much time has passed that I do not recognise her, and I feel overwhelmed with grief at all I have missed out on.

Gabriella is not the only person who is beyond recognition.

After the ceremony, I gather with the rest of the flock of well-wishers around the bridal couple, and wait until Anna sees me.

I open my arms and Anna moves forward to kiss my cheek, her smile warm in response. Then suddenly, her mouth drops open as she realises that the woman standing before her, half my old size, is me. The kiss on the cheek is forgotten as she grabs me in a bear-hug, equal to that of Margaret.

My main fear in staying for the reception had been the need to see and talk to my father. I was scared that I would feel trapped in a similarly distressing pretence as I experienced at Grant and Margaret's wedding, so many years before. Now, as I see my father from a distance, I realise I am not afraid of him. He is no longer the monster who trolled and controlled all my waking and sleeping moments as a child, and who has haunted the decades since. He is just an old man – a very old man – feeble and frail.

This old man starts to move slowly towards the bridal party, and I simply and swiftly move away without acknowledging his presence. Once I would have been stuck on the spot; emotionally and physically trapped. Today, I have the freedom, independence and choice to move to another space, both emotionally and physically.

At that point, I decide that I feel able, and want, to stay for the reception.

I mingle with the other guests and spend time talking to many people I haven't seen in years. Family friends and extended family members express enormous surprise to see me. Over and over, I experience the thrill of not being recognised. Often it takes minutes of conversation before the penny suddenly drops and the exclamation comes, 'Monique, it's you! I didn't even recognise you!'

I know that my physical appearance has changed dramatically, while I strongly suspect that what they also find hard to recognise is the deeper change in my overall demeanour. I feel confident and comfortable in my skin, and I know that this comes across as deeply palpable, even if it is hard for them to define.

I spend time talking to my mother, as we try to find common ground. She asks questions about old friends and colleagues, and I can see that she is trying to find ways of connecting to my life. She also tries to talk to Ryan, awkwardly asking him questions about his work and life. This is the first time I've ever introduced a romantic partner to my family, and I reflect that it must be especially difficult for Mum to know what to say, when the first time she meets my boyfriend is after four years of no contact from me.

Part of me dearly wants to tell Mum how much weight I've lost, yet I resist the drive to do so. There's still a big part of me that longs to hear her express her pride in me, and to feel that I have finally reached the unreachable goal she set for me … to know that I am no longer a disappointment to her. But I also know that telling her about my weight loss success is not the answer. The dynamics between us have never been about my weight. My weight was a smokescreen to obscure the issues that we could never talk about freely.

Ironically, I currently weigh about 10kg more than I did when Mum wrote the letter telling my nineteen-year-old self that I would feel so much better if I lost half of my body, and saying, 'I am telling you *not* to feel guilty in any way that you do not live up to my expectations.'

I find it hard to gauge my mother's feelings as we talk, and I do not know if she feels proud of me. However, it is clear that she is so pleased to see me, and I sense her trying hard to find points of connection, so I want to help facilitate that connection also.

An abiding thought occurs to me as we talk on and off throughout the evening: 'She hasn't changed at all, and that's OK. I have.'

Throughout the wedding reception, my body reminds me that this is a huge event for me. Over the last two years I've had to learn that when I have dizzy spells as a result of my acquired 'postural orthostatic tachycardia syndrome', it's often a sign that I am stressed. During my early weight loss months, I experienced four or five POTS episodes per day; currently they happen only four or five times per week. During the four hours I am at the reception, I have around twenty-five episodes, one every ten minutes or so, lasting up to a minute each time. I am able to 'ride through' most of them without anyone else knowing, but I do end up spilling my drink over Ryan and nearly fainting at the point when we are standing to toast the bride and groom. This reminds me that while in some ways, I am taking this new situation in my stride, it is still a huge effort and stress, and there is a cost that comes along with that. I am very happy to carry that cost; it is stressful nonetheless.

I leave the wedding reception exhausted and elated. Twenty-four hours ago, attendance felt utterly impossible. Many things can change in a short period of time. More to the point, I realise that today was only possible, including my feelings toward both of my parents, because enormous change has been happening inside me, slowly and steadily, at times imperceptibly, for many years now.

Today's events are a tangible sign of these significant changes, while it is hard to recognise the 'me' that has emerged.

Change is a tender dance. When one person shifts, it inevitably affects those around them. The more someone moves and changes, the bigger the effects on others. Movement and change occur both independently from others, and in deep connection with those who matter in our lives.

Finding a home inside my skin has involved both hard work on my part – and unexpected grace from outside myself.

In the days that follow Anna's wedding, I do not find myself at the bottom of the deep psychological hole I had feared.

Rather, I continue the tender dance of change – moving backward and forward – with grace and hope.

Song Download Details & Credits

To download the MP3s for *Inch by Inch*,
Visit: www.inchbyinch.net.au/song-downloads
Password: findinghome

Album Mixed and Mastered by Adrian Hannan 2020 at The SongStore, Victoria, Australia

1. FROZEN

Words and Music © Monique Lisbon 2008

Monique Lisbon:	Vocals and Keyboards
Rod Baker:	Keyboards
Adrian Hannan:	Keyboards
Monica Royal:	'Cello
Lachlan Davidson:	Saxophone
Arrangement/Production:	Rod Baker, Monique Lisbon and Adrian Hannan

2. WASTING AWAY

Words © Monique Lisbon 2014
Music © Adrian Hannan 2019

Monique Lisbon:	Vocals
Adrian Hannan:	Backing vocals, All Instrumentation/ProTools Programming
Arrangement/Production:	Adrian Hannan

3. HEAVY LOAD

Words © Monique Lisbon 2020
Music © Adrian Hannan 2020

Monique Lisbon:	Vocals
Adrian Hannan:	All Instrumentation/ProTools Programming
Arrangement/Production:	Adrian Hannan

4. GOODBYE TO MYSELF

Words and Music © Monique Lisbon 2008

Monique Lisbon:	Vocals
Roger Nicholson:	Piano
Arrangement/Production:	Allan Neuendorf, Monique Lisbon and Adrian Hannan

5. SOLITARY CONFINEMENT

Words © Monique Lisbon 2020
Music © Adrian Hannan 2020

Monique Lisbon:	Vocals
Adrian Hannan:	All Instrumentation/ ProTools Programming
Arrangement/Production:	Adrian Hannan

6. WALK A MILE

Words and Music © Monique Lisbon 2005

Monique Lisbon:	Vocals
Craig Smith:	Piano
Andy Gordon:	Guitar
Tony King:	Double Bass
Rod Wilson:	Drums
Paul Dooley:	Trumpet
Adrian Hannan:	Other Instrumentation/ ProTools Programming
Arrangement/Production:	Monique Lisbon, Allan Neuendorf and Adrian Hannan

7. FREE RENT

Words © Monique Lisbon 2015
Music © Monique Lisbon and Adrian Hannan 2015

Monique Lisbon:	Vocals
Adrian Hannan:	All Instrumentation/ ProTools Programming
Arrangement/Production:	Adrian Hannan

8. TIME

Words and Music © Monique Lisbon and Adrian Hannan 2018

Monique Lisbon:	Vocals
Adrian Hannan:	All Instrumentation/ ProTools Programming
Arrangement/Production:	Adrian Hannan

9. A THOUSAND MILES

Words © Monique Lisbon 2018
Music © Monique Lisbon and Adrian Hannan 2018
'The journey of a thousand miles …' quotation by Lao Tzu

Monique Lisbon:	Vocals
Adrian Hannan:	Backing vocals, All Instrumentation/ ProTools Programming
Arrangement/Production:	Adrian Hannan

10. DELIBERATELY

Words and Music © Monique Lisbon 2005
after Henry David Thoreau (1817-1862)

Monique Lisbon:	Vocals
Roger Nicholson:	Piano
Spike Avery:	Bass
Rod Wilson:	Drums
Adrian Hannan:	All Other Instrumentation/ ProTools Programming
Arrangement/Production:	Allan Neuendorf, Monique Lisbon and Adrian Hannan

11. ME AND YOU

Words © Monique Lisbon 2019
Music © Monique Lisbon and Adrian Hannan 2019

Monique Lisbon:	Vocals
Adrian Hannan:	Backing vocals, All Instrumentation ProTools Programming
Arrangement/Production:	Adrian Hannan

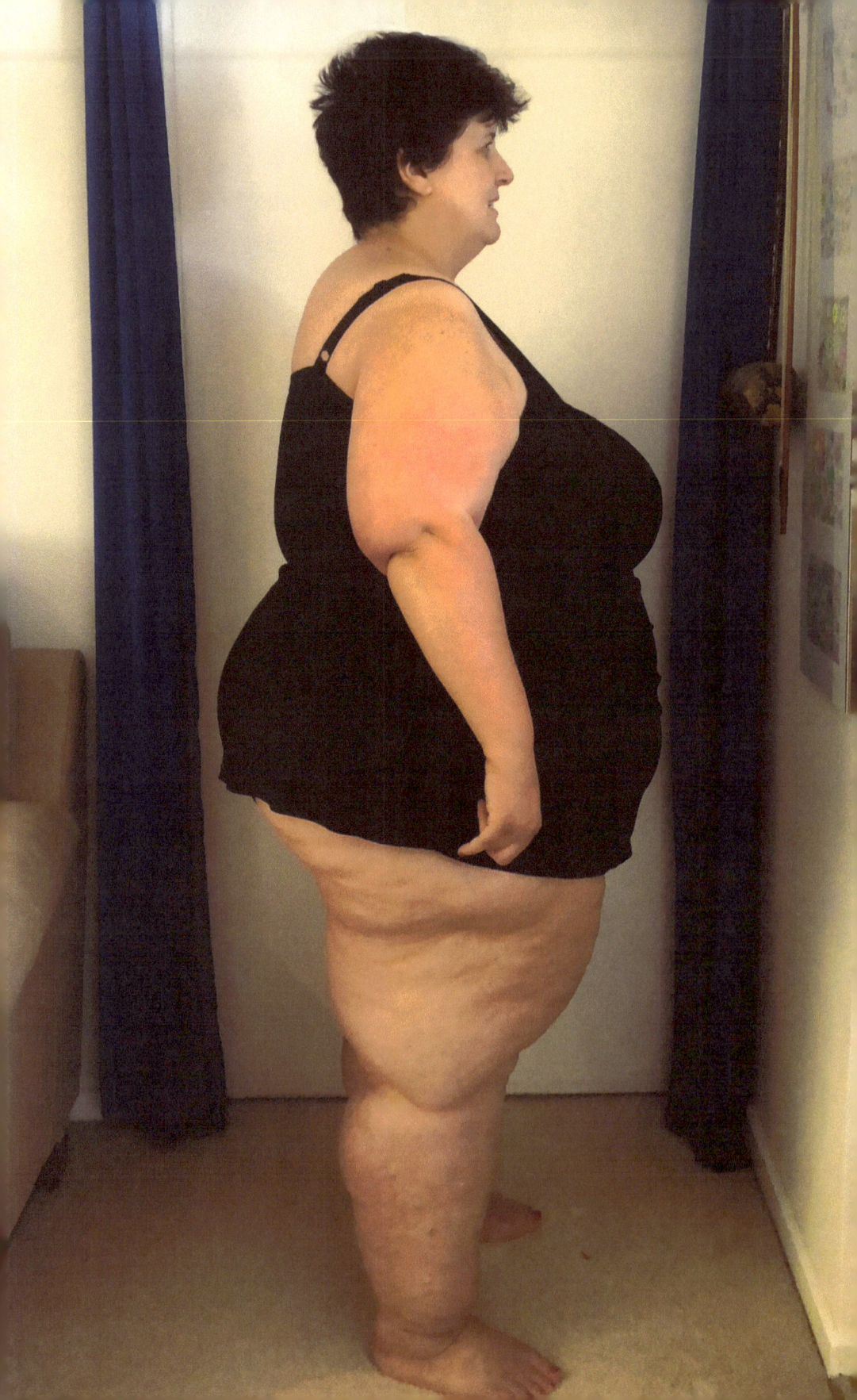

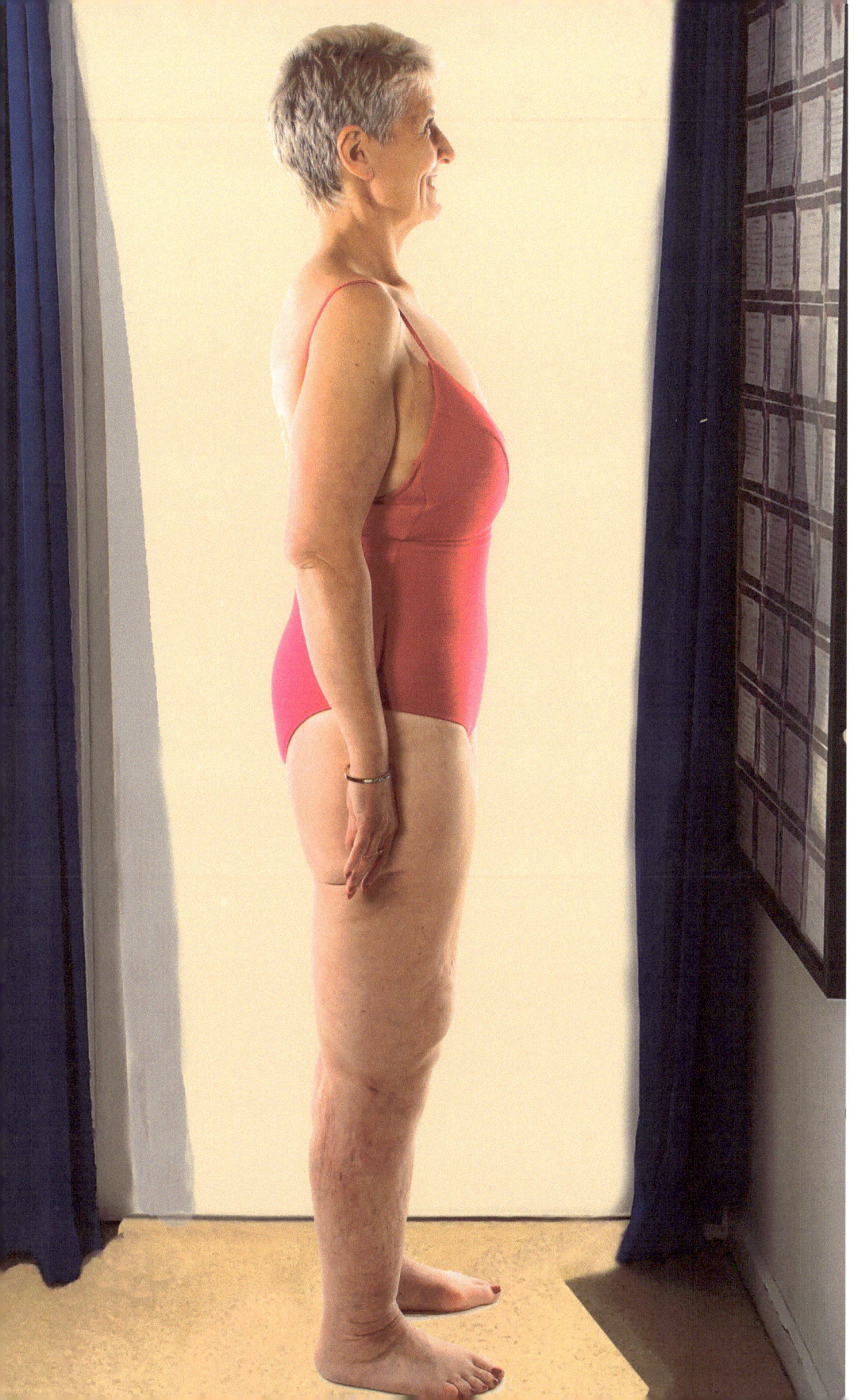

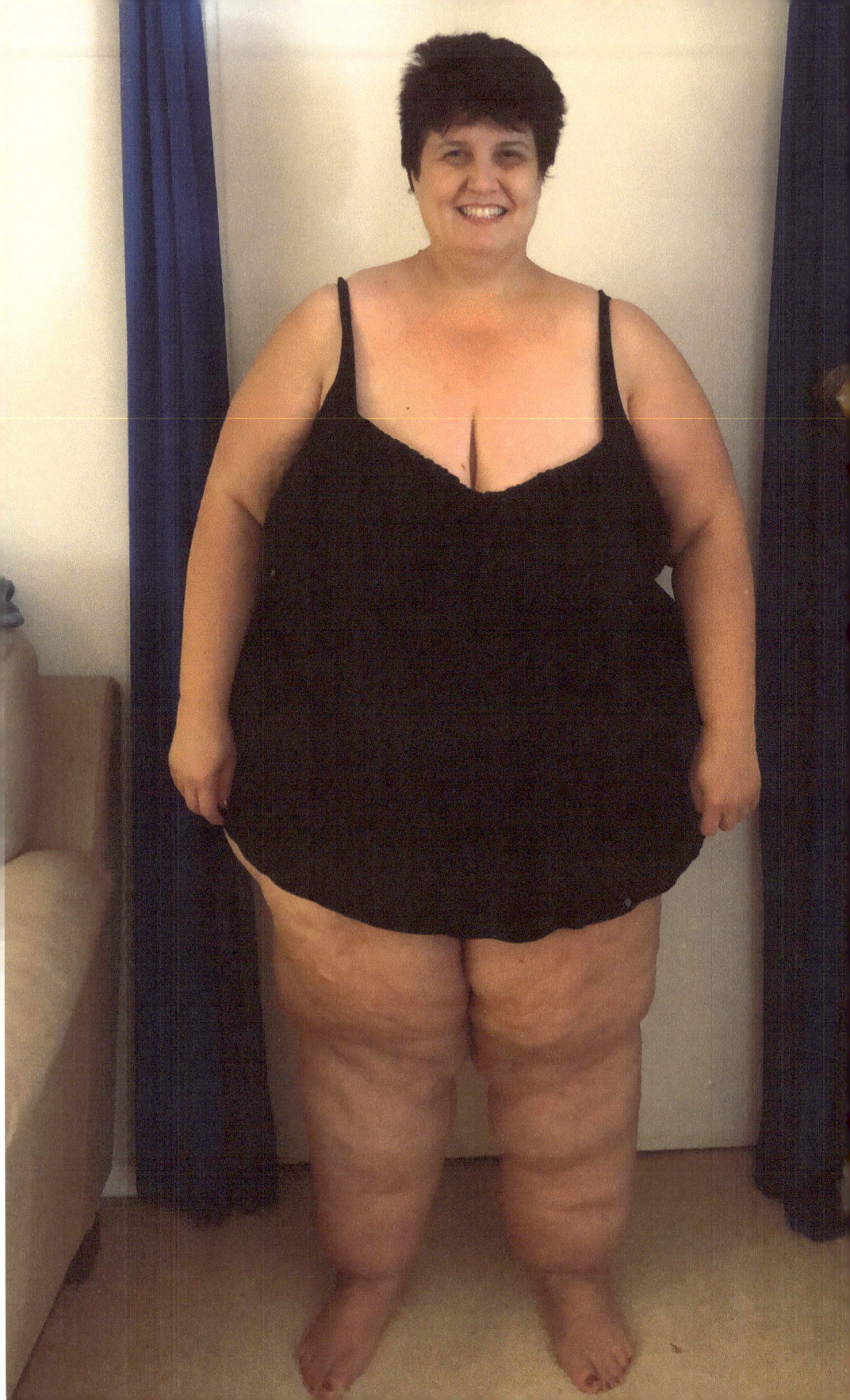

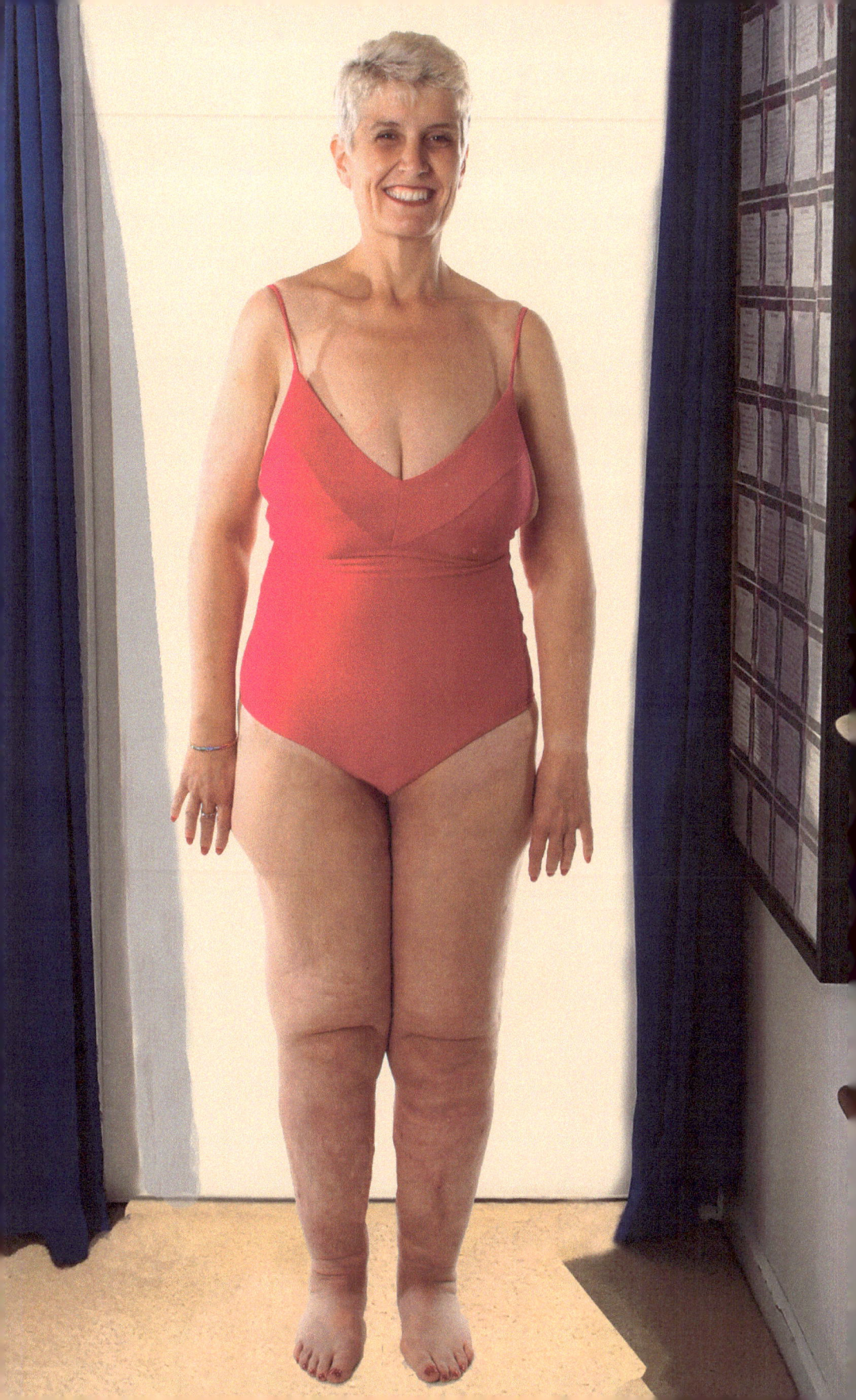

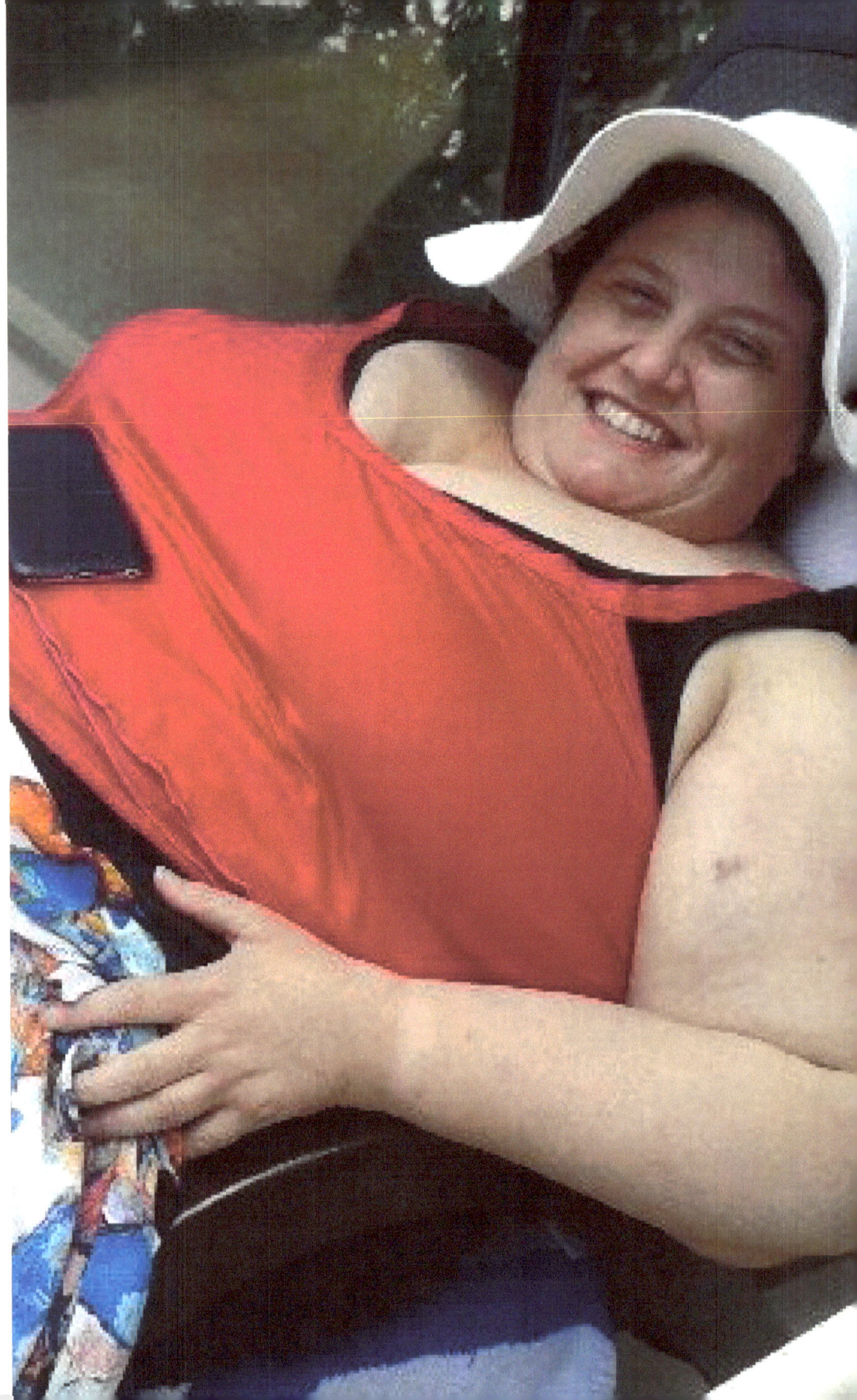

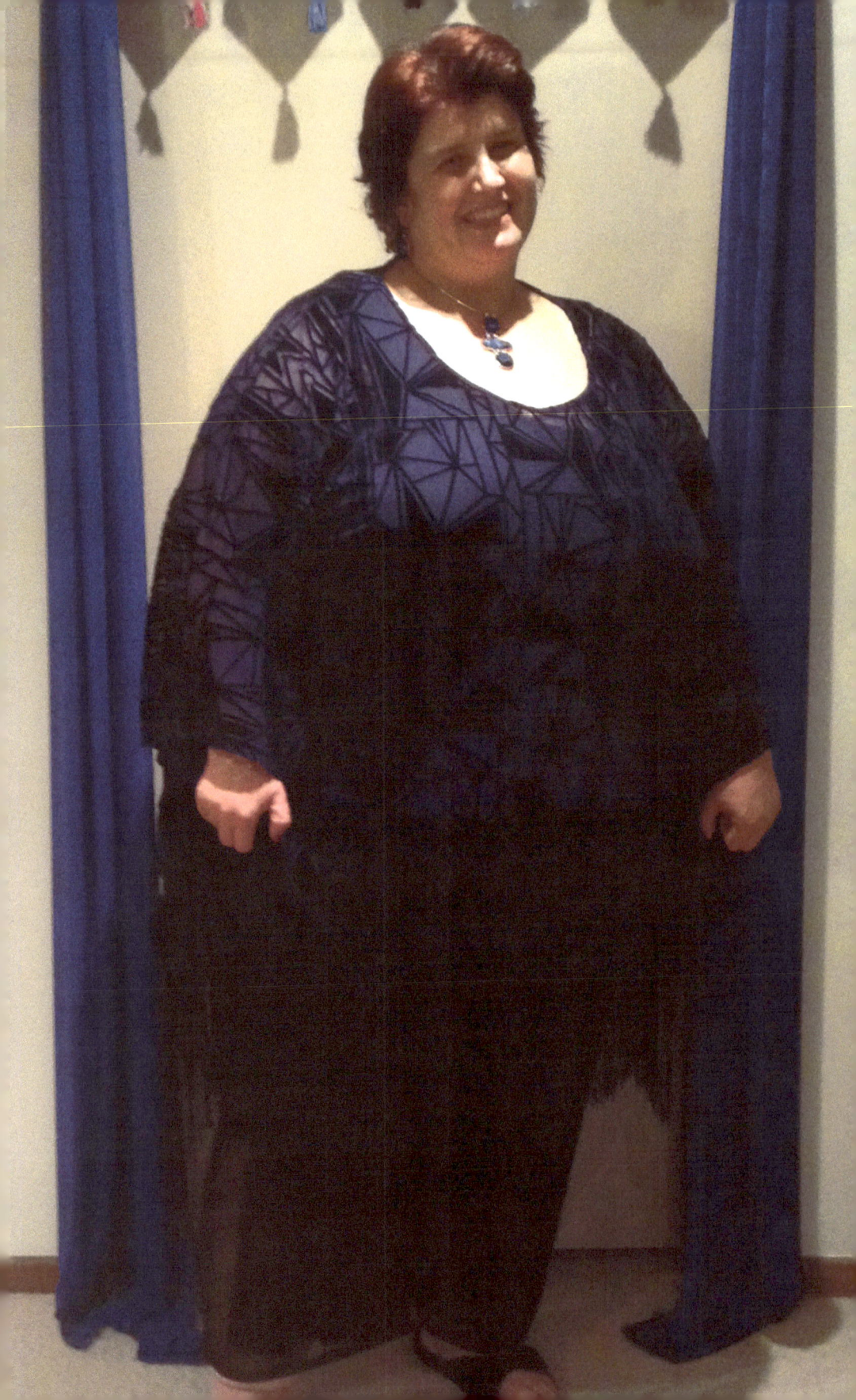

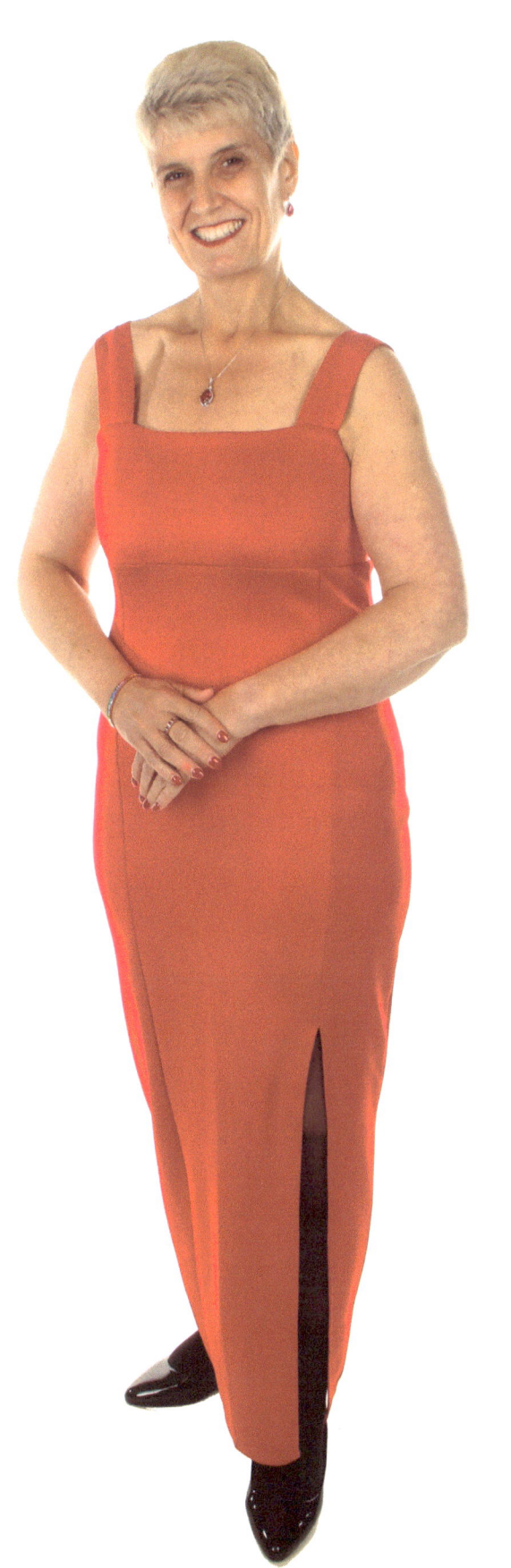

www.ingramcontent.com/pod-product-compliance
Lightning Source LLC
Chambersburg PA
CBHW041503010526
44107CB00049B/1631